HEALERS
HARMED&
HARMFUL

CONRAD W. WEISER

HEALERS
HARMED&
HARMFUL

FORTRESS PRESS / MINNEAPOLIS

HEALERS—HARMED AND HARMFUL

Scripture quotations unless otherwise noted are from the New Revised Standard Version Bible, copyright © 1989 by the Division of Christian Education of the National Council of the Churches of Christ in the United States.

Cover design: James Brisson

Library of Congress Cataloging-in-Publication Data

Weiser, Conrad
    Healers—harmed and harmful / Conrad W. Weiser.
      p. cm.
    Includes bibliographical references and index.
    ISBN 0-8006-2630-3 (alk. paper)
    1. Clergy—Psychology. 2. Laity—Psychology. 3. Organizational
behavior. 4. Defense mechanisms (Psychology)—Religious aspects—
Christianity. I. Title.
    BV4398.W45 1994
253.5'2—dc20   94-9987
                                         CIP

The paper used in this publication meets the minimum requirements of American National Standard for Information Sciences—Permanence of Paper for Printed Library Materials, ANSI Z329.48-1984. ∞™

Manufactured in the U.S.A.   AF 1-2630

98   97   96   95   94   1   2   3   4   5   6   7   8   9   10

CONTENTS

90276

PREFACE

Rollo May published in *The Art of Counseling* (1938) his vision that one day clergy and related helping professionals would engage in an intensive program of psychotherapy as part of their training and preparation. This vision, he thought, would become accepted practice within only a few years (May 1967, 165–67). Such a proposal was an obvious solution to the need for the development of a mature body of clergy. This practice for clergy in training has not happened.

A program of intensive psychodynamic psychotherapy can assist in restructuring toward a wholeness in which the professional emerges wounded but well. My own finding is that those clergy who are among the most successful in mainline churches report almost unanimously that they have experienced significant personal trauma. Seventy percent of these clergy have participated in some form of intensive personal psychotherapy, compared to fewer than 15 percent of clergy with less successful career tracks. To May's work I shall add the later pioneering work of Otto Kernberg and Heinz Kohut, who changed the way psychoanalysis conceptualizes human development.

This book explores the factors that can lead a religious professional either to become depressed or to interact with others in inappropriate ways. Moreover, congregations act to provoke and sustain conditions that can further endanger religious professionals. These need careful attention from theorists and counselors alike.

Damaged professionals damage others. When damaged clergy are linked to damaged systems, the results can be catastrophic. The portrait of these harmed professionals and those they harm is a dark and convoluted one. This book attempts to bring some conceptual and practical clarity to these convolutions using the tools and theoretical frames of dynamic and analytic psychology.

Psychodynamic and psychoanalytic psychology present models of human development and group functioning which emphasize the power of the unconscious and the defensive structures ("shells" designed for protection, constructed around the self) erected early in life in reaction to parental interferences with the normal developmental process. These forces are then manifested in academic performance, relationship formation, career choice, and nearly every other facet of life and decision making.

Unconscious drives and impulses cause us to perceive the distorted rather than the real and become especially visible in situations where religious professionals are in crisis. This book examines the manifestations of the irrational, the emotional, the primitive, and the bizarre that exist in the everyday life of professionals and groups within church systems.

Terms from psychodynamic and analytic therapy will be used throughout this book, but they will be defined and illustrated. Psychoanalytic theory will be applied to the personalities and the work of church professionals, to their mutual interaction, and to their interaction with congregations. The effects of unconscious primary or primitive processes will be examined as they are detected in both usual and exceptional behavior among individuals and groups found in ecclesiastical systems. Primary or *primitive process* is the powerful content of our dreams, the dark and unspoken fears and drives that are often loaded with sexual or aggressive desires for pleasure, attachment, safety, and the avoidance of pain or discomfort. Primitive or primary process has no time, no limits, and no chronology. Reason has no part.

Although many of my illustrations come from clergy and congregations, the themes of this book also apply to professional counselors and lay professionals, especially when they are working in relatively isolated contexts. Most importantly, this book is for all persons who feel called upon or drawn to caregiving or counseling as a profession. Each professional has the potential to interact with people and congregations and therefore to worsen the condition of the total system. When a damaged professional interacts with healthy persons and systems, that health itself is threatened, disrupted, and potentially destroyed.

The seeds of this project grew out of my evolving disenchantment with personal and professional growth models. For fifteen years I maintained one central professional goal: to design and implement education and growth experiences for religious professionals and their intimates which would enable their work to be more effective, their relationships to be more intimate, and their lives to be more hopeful. Despite this, however, I saw religious professionals who professed a noteworthy value base, a high commitment to the tasks, and all the requisite training, fail or get into trouble in high proportions. I witnessed the disastrous results of failed intimate relationships. I wondered why congregations that claimed to respond to sound planning and interim intervention failed to be faithful to their mission or to achieve their stated goals.

These failures resulted from the distortions in perception that were driven by unresolved material in these individuals and systems. A new goal emerged. My goal now is to make religious professionals and congregational systems conscious of the presence and power of the unconscious as a driving force in relationships, decision making, and all other aspects of their work. It surprises me that many religious systems and still more professionals who deal in mystery and myth seem unable to affirm the presence of forces within themselves that lie beyond consciousness and yet are actively at work in their lives.

Two caveats need to be entered. First, this is not another book about clergy sex abuse. Clergy sexual abuse, along with the devastation of its victims and the betrayal of congregations and church systems, is certainly a worthy subject and has been well presented by several authors, such as Marie Fortune and Peter Rutter. This book will, however, set abuse into its developmental context as a consequence of early damage inflicted by parents and a process of internalizing this damage. The premise of this book is that the harmful or inappropriate actions of the adult are a product of unprocessed damage from childhood. The picture drawn here is intended to be a more encompassing one.

Second, clergy and others seeking a ready-made therapeutic how-to for restructuring the self will not find it here. This book can identify basic ways to explore what has motivated persons to pursue a religious or counseling profession, and it will help them detect when they or their colleagues are potentially in trouble.

Special acknowledgment for whatever maturity I have achieved is due in part to therapists, supervisors, and mentors who have been a major part of my personal unconsciousness-raising. I also acknowledge the contribution of my patients, who have taught me about always paying attention. Three persons deserve special acknowledgment. Marjorie Hunt and Timothy Staveteig have read, reread, and suggested rewriting alternatives that helped me shape a readable text. Marjorie's love of words, care for the language, and support for this book, coupled with Timothy's respect for the structural integrity of books and his persuasive pushing, have taught me at last to construct sentences, paragraphs, and chapters in ways that communicate their intent. And finally, I thank Barbara Holmberg for her intimate partnership over the last decade.

INTRODUCTION:
PLUNGING IN

Picture a typical candidacy committee, perhaps for a judicatory board or a seminary. Each committee member at this meeting feels constrained by at least two considerations: First, each wants the approved candidates to succeed in professional religious work and, second, each knows that a dire need exists for competent professionals to fill the jobs. The committee is composed of members with a variety of concerns and interests. Some represent teaching faculty or the judicatory office. Others are working religious professionals who have had experience working with students. Still others represent broader constituencies in the decision process. Each member of the committee brings a combination of commitment, experience, and caution to the task.

Prior to the meeting each member has reviewed files for each of three candidates. In accordance with the committee process, Martha, an active participant in a large congregation, has been assigned to present three candidates at this meeting. She has also been asked to monitor the question period for each candidate. If any committee member should seek further information, Martha will contact the candidate for the information.

Martha has been involved with religious work for many years and has worked at a thriving counseling center supported by her congregation and others in the region. Derrick is the first candidate she introduces. His background is rather typical: He has grown up in an upper-middle-class home with professional parents and is the oldest child in his family. His academic record is quite good, and he is also a musician. Derrick has been involved in a congregation for much of his life.

Derrick has glowing recommendations from college faculty and former spiritual mentors. It appears to Martha that Derrick has been successful at everything he has attempted. His application states that he has a strong desire to challenge the shortcomings of the denomination and participate in changing some of the disastrous social situations of the world. As the data unfold, the committee clearly becomes impressed with Derrick. David, a long-time member of the committee, asks whether Derrick believes he can change the world. Derrick says that he believes he can. David smiles and tells Derrick that he predicts Derrick will modify this grand vision when he has been in the profession a few years. Endorsement is granted.

Dan, the second candidate, quickly elicits sympathy from Martha and several other committee members. He was raised from the age of thirteen by his sister and her husband following the death of their invalid mother. His father had died of a destroyed liver when Dan was eight. Dan's application presents supportive recommendations from religious professionals who worked with him during his adolescent years when he was a better-than-average student. He seems strongly motivated to join the clergy. The committee endorses his candidacy.

To present Gail, the third candidate, is Martha's greatest joy. Gail is well grounded and seems quite secure, so that Martha can imagine her as a competent and caring practitioner. Gail is older than the other candidates. She had been a successful history teacher at the high school level for ten years, but wants to connect her three greatest interests: teaching, helping people, and serving her church. Her experience and apparent maturity make her an easy candidate to endorse.

The mix of candidates seen before this committee is rather typical. Each one has apparent strengths to bring to a religious profession. But each of these candidates is vulnerable, apt to behave in ways that may damage themselves and others. The predicaments of these candidates and others like them are traced throughout this book as they move from demonstrating vulnerability, to becoming at risk, and then to crisis.

PROFESSIONALS AT RISK

A high proportion of pastoral counselors, clergy, counselors, social workers, and therapists are at risk for future difficulty. The attraction of less-than-fully functioning persons to religious professions is not new, but two factors are new: First, the roles of religious professionals can now be viewed differently; second, religious professionals are often less amenable to change.

Being *at risk* is a combination of the professional's personality structure and environmental factors, such as the effects of poor choices in marriage or peer relationships, interaction with a difficult and resistant congregation, or social isolation. Environmental factors may be influenced by distorted personal decision making, but the interaction of personality structure and environment is potentially toxic. These forces can come together and drive a professional to *act out* (interact with others in inappropriate ways) or *act in* (become depressed). An at-risk personality structure permits functioning of only limited complexity. When the perimeters of the complexity are breached, when internal needs and external demands push the self to the limits of its range, then the professional can no longer function and is likely to become depressed or to act out. Because of increasing pressure and complexity in the life process, primitive pieces of the self burst through, shattering the defensive structure and disabling the professional.

Developmental damage inflicted upon the child by inappropriate parental action or inaction inhibits normal development and distorts perception of reality. Inhibited development and the resulting distortions come together to become *dysfunction* in which clear perceptions of reality, the ability to distinguish the boundaries of the self and those of others, ability to establish effective intimate relationships, and intellectual functioning are impeded. Of all the factors that interfere with successful ministry, personal developmental damage is perhaps the most common and the most often ignored (or, more accurately, denied). Developmental damage often goes unmentioned and unaddressed until the actions of clergy become embarrassing or scandalous. When this happens, a manifestation is often treated as the problem rather than as the symptom of a more profound injury.

Dynamic and analytic psychology map an individual's development from birth through adulthood and provide definitions of small- and large-group interaction. Each recognizes the power of *unconscious forces* (motivation originating beyond the level of awareness). Together these psychologies provide an understanding of developmental damage and are able to address and treat it. These models can enable the psychology of the church to be as mature as its theology.

Traditional prevention models—such as ones that seek to help leaders to establish a balance between work and family or to maintain appropriate professional distance and thereby avoid inappropriate sexual contact or work more effectively in staff systems—are largely ineffective for those religious or healing professionals who are already at risk or who have a demonstrated vulnerability. These models fail for the same reasons that admonitions such as "just say no" and "you don't have to feel that way" are ineffective for endangered individuals. At-risk professionals are not very aware that they are potentially in trouble; they believe themselves to be acting and performing appropriately. Such prevention models are aimed at an audience that is presumed to be healthier than it actually is.

Prevention models cannot break through or correct well-established perception distortions and defensive structures that existed long before the church professional joined the clergy. Indeed, these defensive structures may have led to the decision to enter a church profession. Such a decision was the manifestation of an unconscious drive to belong at last to a caring system or a perfect system, or to become important, or to help others to help the self; or the decision may have grown out of the fears of living without controls or from a variety of other unconscious motivations. Later, a similar, unconsciously perceived lack of satisfaction most often leads clergy and other church professionals to act out or become depressed. To declare church professionals to be unique only amplifies defenses rather than corrects them.

Often the reasons cited for professionals becoming at risk include increased pressure on clergy in the form of greater or more diverse expectations from clients, congregations, or sponsoring agencies. At one time, the result of such pressures was termed *burnout*. Burnout is not a fruitful description, however, because it names the symptom and not the underlying condition. The symptom called *burnout* is the result of a breakdown of the defensive structure developed by the individual early in life as a protection from others and from the self and its accompanying depression.

High proportions of professional populations are psychologically damaged and at risk. My experience suggests it may be as high as 30 percent, but a more defendable figure is 25 percent. Clergy are part of this population (*Encyclopedia of Social Work* 1987, *American Psychologist* 1991, *American Journal of Psychiatry* 1990). The percentage of at-risk clergy is commensurate with that of other professional populations, including physicians, psychologists, teachers, attorneys, corporate executives, and academics. A rule of thirds is often invoked to describe a given population. About one-third of any population is at risk at any given time. Of those, one-third have moved beyond being at risk and are already in trouble.

The literature about church professionals or congregations often presents health as the predominant condition and makes sickness or dysfunction the exception. The truth seems darker—in fact, the data indicate the reverse. As life-stage theoreticians have indicated over the last few decades, change—not stability—is the norm, and change moves toward dysfunction and disequilibrium, not toward health. Figure 1 (p. 5) depicts the research on clergy, including the population examined and the conclusions drawn.

Figure 1: Mental Health Studies of Clergy

A summary of studies regarding the relative mental health of clergy or clergy candidates appears in C. D. Batson and W. L. Ventis. "Mental Health or Sickness," *The Religious Experience: A Social-Psychological Perspective* (New York: Oxford University Press, 1982), Chapter 7.

Author	Sample Population	Findings
Dunn (1965)	Religious Professionals (Catholic)	Religious professionals more perfectionistic, insecure, withdrawn, and socially inept
Lindskoog and Kirk (1975)	45 Protestant seminary students	No relationship between any of the measures of religious involvement and self-actualization
Rank (1955)	800 male Protestant theological students	Conservative religious attitudes and belief were positively correlated with authoritarianism
Rank (1961)	800 male Protestant theological students	Conservatively religious were both more dependent and more submissive
Roe (1956)	Seminary students and students of other professions	Seminary students are more neurotic than students of other professions
Strunk (1959)	60 preministerial and 50 business students	Preministerial students were more aggressive
Webster (1967)	191 Protestant seminarians	Seminarians poorer in mental health than nonclergy
Webster (1967)	191 Protestant seminary students compared with nonseminary norms	Seminarians scored lower on self-actualization than nonseminarians

If one-quarter to one-third of the clergy are at risk or operating at less than mature levels, then each congregation served by this portion of the professional population will remain in or move toward immaturity. Five to seven years are needed for a congregation to grow and heal after an inadequate ministry. If the average length of a ministry in one place is seven years or less, then at any point in time as many as 60 percent of all parishes are dysfunctional or potentially so—no small systemic issue. Mature pastors can spend most of their time cleaning up dysfunction and immaturity in parish after parish in an endless circle. What clergyperson wants to undertake the task of establishing healthy functioning while knowing that this congregation has a two-out-of-three chance of becoming dysfunctional again? It is as if healthy pastors are window washers who create a clear vision for only brief periods of time until the glass becomes clouded and distorted again.

PERSPECTIVES

Several considerations that delineate the biases of this book are necessary before we proceed.

Individual and Systems Thinking

Any discussion of clergy dysfunction alone or congregational dysfunction alone is incomplete. The two go together and shape each other. Therefore, two languages need to be spoken: the language of individual psychology and the language of systems. The psychodynamic processes of the congregational system are affected by and have an effect upon the individual psychodynamics of the religious professional.

As adults become what they are as a result of childhood interaction with their parents, so the parents develop in part because of the influence of the child. This interaction happens within a highly circumstantial context. In a like manner, religious systems in 1940 were far different from what they will be in the year 2000. Each context issues distinctive expectations for religious professionals. But the same psychological events are happening for individuals and systems, whether it be in 1940 or 2000. Psychology then tries to define human and systems development in universal terms, much like theology, philosophy, and literature. Psychology seeks to answer three questions: First, what is the nature of human beings? Second, how do they become the way they are? Third, how do they live together?

The language of individual psychology concerns itself with the way the child incorporates messages received from the parent and with the dysfunction that these messages may cause. The language of systems deals with the psychodynamics of people in groups. A system has a life that is different from the aggregate lives of the individuals who comprise it. For example, a system insists upon certain behaviors and styles for its membership. When a religious professional complains that something is wrong in a congregation, he or she may be indicating that something is personally amiss. When a congregation complains about the clergyperson, something may be amiss with them. Most often, something is wrong with both.

Corporations, academic institutions, medical and governmental or military systems are similar to religious ones. The individuals who are part of these systems are expected to comply with the culture of the systems and, when this does not happen, the individual is perceived as being at fault. Often that which is perceived as individual pathology is actually systemic dysfunction. Anne Wilson Schaef and Diane Fassel (1988) claim that we are a culture of dysfunctional systems. Some American therapists even engage in a form of lifestyle therapy that equates cultural norms with health and takes as its goal helping people to do and desire whatever the majority seem to do and desire. I believe that we are more dysfunctional now than we used to be.

Trait Not State

A *trait* is a stable condition that manifests itself in healthy or unhealthy ways throughout adult life. Traits are manifested particularly when life is threatened or becomes too complex. A *state* is an observable characteristic or behavior that emerges as a result of conditions. States are an aberrant function and not part of the fabric of the individual. If clergy and congregational dysfunction are based on states, then skills and knowledge may be capable of altering them. If they are trait-based, then no amount of skill training or workshops will alter the dysfunction. State-based psychology is more behavioral and excludes an unconscious. Most leaders in religious systems want to believe that individuals and subgroups within the system are dealing with states and not traits. Commonly overlooked are the deeper, darker components of personality and systems structures.

The problems of clergy, congregations, and religious systems are most often the result of a condition. These problems reflect the trait of the individual or the system and are not separate events, occurrences, or behaviors. Plugging the holes in the dike, treating systems as if they are conditions, is often a chosen intervention stategy. But the condition of the dike itself is not examined. Plugging holes takes great energy, postpones analysis, and seduces us into believing that we are at least doing something to save the city.

At best, people choose a religious profession for mixed reasons. Although I would like to think that people could have purely mature and uncontaminated reasons for choosing a religious career, I have never seen that happen any more than I have seen a new marriage grounded solely in reality.

The Context

Counseling with numerous clergy, doing interim ministry within congregations, and listening to judicatory officials has yielded a rather similar impression. The religious climate of America is changing, and the change, reflected in lowered congregational membership, reduced system income, and a shortage of high-quality professional leaders, is likely a permanent one. Previously, American congregations could ignore flurries of interest in human rights and the environment, but now these global concerns affect the future of the human race and demand the concern of religious systems. Unless mainstream religion is adequately involved, its irrelevance will be hastened.

Religious professionals once had high status in the community, but this has not been so for at least a generation. As one priest recently remarked, we now have negative status. The quality of persons attracted to the mainline ministry is declining and may correlate to the declining status of the profession. In addition, career disenchantment is affecting the majority of clergypersons. More clergy seem to be leaving than are entering—at least across the spectrum of mainstream Western religion: priest, pastor, rabbi.

The membership of many mainline churches seems to have become both entrenched and survival-oriented. Members want to hold on to what they have and are reluctant to risk the status quo for the new. While religious communities have always tended to cling to the past, the forces to stay the same have become exaggerated and little chance of change seems probable in the foreseeable future. Edwin H. Friedman (1985) discusses the terrorist tactics of subgroups within the remaining membership of mainline religious bodies who attempt to hold the rest of the membership hostage until the subgroup gets what it wants. The practice of voting with feet and pocketbooks continues.

Signs of change are visible in congregations and pastors; it is often unclear what the direction and scope of that change is. Some clergy state that they do not know who or what they are anymore, and many congregations seem equally unclear about themselves or their mission.

Economic changes have further affected religious systems. Lowered income and declining interest among members of congregations have lowered the religious system's income potential. The increasing costs of programs and personnel, coupled with lowered congregational income, have placed limitations on the creative, challenging, and compassionate outreach of the system. Controversy is avoided for fear of alienating any portion of the active, contributing membership and thus further lowering income. Freud (1921) wrote that when a profession or system has its own survival as its primary goal, the risk of extinction is present.

Attempts to be inclusive, while laudable, may also further complicate. The more inclusive the membership, the more vague its nature or identity. Membership has always been rooted in exclusiveness. We know who we are in part through knowing what others are not. Exclusiveness makes clear who is in and who is out, but exclusive systems are not necessarily strong, nor do they or should they survive. Exclusiveness is rather the precondition for, and not a guarantor of, strength and survival. Witness the eating clubs of Princeton or the fraternal societies which flourished during the first half of the century. As long as a society tolerated the exclusiveness of sex as a membership criterion, these groups were strong and alive.

Changing language expectations and terms of reference further complicate the context. Ecclesiastical jargon has long since lost its power. In an attempt to be inclusive and inoffensive, ecclesiastical language often becomes bland, vague, and clumsy. Words and phrases in this linguistic transition lack a sense of the concrete and immediate. I recently read a protest document for a major denomination in which the complete phrase "persons of color with a primary language other than English" appeared with numbing repetition. The intended force of the document was dulled by the recurrent use of this phrase. Even the term *clergy*, which excludes lay religious professionals, is often replaced by the term *caregivers*, which carries a negative connotation in any twelve-step program, or by *helpers*, which is too inclusive to describe the set-apart role of clergy. These recent changes in membership, status, and concern for language have altered the context and played a part in determining what kind of person may be driven to seek the professional ministry as a career.

The Spectrum of Dysfunction

Dysfunction is not an on-or-off switch but a continuum that exists in degrees. Because nearly all parents damage their children, almost no one grows up unscathed. The healthier or more mature the parents, the healthier the children. A professional once at risk need not always remain so. Therapy often succeeds in dealing with the issues that created an at-risk condition before the damage bursts through. Maturation takes time. The strength of our own defenses and the degree of damage we have sustained determine that some of us require longer than others to mature.

A story is told about Abraham Maslow that ought to be true even if it is not. Late in his career, before leaving on a lecture tour, he told his students that he was going on a quest for a living self-actualized person (his term for mature). He knew that he himself was not one. When asked on his return, he told his students that he met two self-actualized people. Both were over sixty-five and both were boring. The story supports a popular notion that neurosis is interesting. It also points to the fact that maturing is a process that is never completed.

Religious systems attract dysfunctional persons in part because these systems seem to offer a kind of caring that cannot otherwise be found in these persons' lives. An increasing number of clergy have been abused as children. An even greater percentage come from some sort of dys-functional family. Even many candidates looking for a second career in a religious profession seem to have been dissatisfied or unsuccessful in their first career. Some of these are looking for something magical that the world has so far denied them.

The Clergy

The clergy who illustrate examples in this book can be assumed to be bright, well trained professionally, and well motivated. Most of them want to be satisfied in their work. They are mainline clergy—priests, rabbis, and pastors—who have completed at least one professional degree beyond their undergraduate degree and are firmly in the upper 25 percent of the intelligence range.

Clergy wish to be considered unique. But the desire for uniqueness is not found only among religious professionals. Physicians, psychologists, attorneys, and many other professionals also claim to be unique. Indeed, in some respects each profession really is unique. Unique to the helping professions, for example, are the extremely high ethical and moral ex-pectations laid upon their practitioners and the high costs to career of ignoring them. Some breaches threaten careers more than others do. The costs of poor preaching, social inappropriateness, or general ineptness are minimal. Sexual acting out or abuse, however, usually ends a career.

One area in which the religious professional is not unique is in career dissatisfaction. Surveys of physicians, teachers, and psychologists who have been in their profession for twenty-five years or more report that 70 percent would choose a different career if they had to choose again. Not even professionals in general are unique when it comes to dissatisfaction. Studs Terkel (1974) reported that 80 percent of all Americans did not like their work, regardless of the job.

But why is dysfunction so high among the bright and capable group that constitutes the professional population? Certain kinds of dysfunction seem to characterize the professional person. Because they are both bright and highly motivated, professionals adopt certain varieties of defensive structures that tend to put them at risk.

The Congregation

A congregation is conceptually more akin to a community than to a family. Like any community, a congregation has an identity of its own. It also has requirements for membership and offers a range of involvement from intense to minimal. The least involved congregational members are likely to use clergy, other congregation members, and church facilities for ritual purposes only. Many members of a congregation may see the religious community as little more than a photo-op location available for the rare occasions in life, such as weddings, when social expectation requires it.

Congregations modeled or built on the family continue to exist, but in increasingly smaller numbers. In rare small social communities parents and children of several families over several generations are bound together through intermarriage and constitute a congregation. In these systems an occasional outsider marries into the family, refreshing the gene pool from a neighboring "tribe." The newcomer is welcomed only if he or she abides by the rules of the closed system.

Congregations, both community and family-systems models, have had histories of their own. Each has a core personality susceptible to distortion. Their reactions tend to be as much magical as based in reality. Congregations quickly establish myths and beliefs about themselves. These beliefs are often quite different from those that are voiced.

DEFENSIVE STRUCTURES

Part Two (chapters 5 through 8) describes and discusses defensive structures in their pure form, a form in which they seldom manifest themselves. This approach, which clarifies each structure and does not alter the concept of the universality of the defensive style mix, has been chosen for clarity of presentation, even at the risk of overlooking the similarities between styles.

The egocentricity of the narcissist (chapter 5), the rigidity of the compulsive (chapter 6), and the passive neediness, indecisiveness, and manipulation of the depressed/dependent personality (chapter 7) are symptoms of an injury. Most religious professionals, however, are apt to judge these actual symptoms as the only issues to be addressed.

Two elements need to be kept in mind: First, variations in the level of function and a mixture of defensive styles can be observed among religious professionals; second, these defensive structures, and not merely the professional lapses, need to be addressed. Finally, a new defensive structure appears to have emerged among religious professionals, and this needs attention by those whose professional judgments are based on more long-standing styles.

Variations in Defensive Structures

In reality one structure seldom exists alone or in complete purity. Yet for the at-risk religious professional, personal and family history combine to set the stage for future difficulty. Even though the level of stress that an individual defensive structure can tolerate before it breaks down is not clearly known, each damaged and at-risk professional is a kind of time bomb. Trouble will come eventually, when the person can no longer maintain adequate levels of energy to sustain the defensive structure at a functional level. These will interact in kairotic time, when the time is right, to explode or implode. An acting out is a mini-explosion, and an acting in is a mini-implosion. One or both may occur along the way as the at-risk person moves inexorably toward increasing professional and personal dysfunction.

After the acting out or acting in has occurred, a religious professional is clearly in trouble. Such an episode needs to be followed by a process of crisis intervention during which a new person other than the publicly known professional is gradually revealed.

Judicatory officials in religious systems need to know candidates' life stories, not to exclude at-risk candidates from the profession, but rather to judge the potential interventions that may be required early in professional careers. Candidates for religious professions—feeling, as most of them do, called by God—cannot but perceive those who question their developmental needs and their professional risk to be blocking God's will. The potential for confrontation is amplified when the one-third of those candidates who are at risk is matched with the one-third of their examiners who are at risk as well.

People use defensive structures to greater and lesser degrees. When a person has a high level of defensiveness, his or her functioning will be considered low. That is, this person's perception of reality will be strongly distorted by his or her defensive structure. Therapists and others will have a difficult time in relating to this person because his or her worldview (informed by these defensive structures) is significantly different from that of an average person.

A person with only a moderate level of defensive structure is probably functioning at a higher level and is able to see most things as others do. It is also possible for high-functioning narcissists, compulsives, or depressed/dependent persons to have confused and unsatisfactory intimate lives and yet function professionally with some success. Therefore, these chapters observe that moderate defensive structure levels suggest the possibility of high functioning, whereas high levels of a defensive structure suggest lower functioning. The lower the level of defensive structure, the higher the level of function, and the more possible a successful intervention is.

Depressed/Dependent

Each chapter in Part Two contains the official definition (from the American Psychiatric Association, *Diagnostic and Statistical Manual of Mental Disorders—Third Edition Revised* [1987], hereafter the DSM III-R) of each defensive style. The exception is the depressed/dependent defensive structure, a composite of two structures that I have observed frequently in tandem. The reader is encouraged to read through and beyond the definitions, which have the rigidity of all professional definitions.

When I first began my work with clergy, only two styles manifested themselves clearly among this group, the narcissist and the compulsive, along with an interesting combination of the two in almost equal parts. In the last decade, a third defensive style—depressed/dependent—has appeared increasingly among the ranks of clergy.

The greatest proportion of religious professionals are a combination of the narcissistic and the compulsive. The next highest proportion are compulsive, and the third, narcissistic. The fourth highest in number are the depressed/dependent. Fewest in number, and the most problematic, are the borderlines. Only a few borderlines make it to a theological school, where they can pose difficulties for fellow students and faculty alike, and fewer of these actually join the full time ranks of clergy. Persons with this defensive structure are without question the most difficult with which religious systems have to deal.

PART ONE

JUST BELOW THE SURFACE

THE RISKINESS
OF CHILDHOOD

Children, at birth, are not just a collection of uncontrolled impulses, but small creatures with the full capacity for emotional development and maturity. Each child needs two emotional gifts from its parents: self-esteem and self-confidence. *Self-esteem* involves feeling positive about oneself; *self-confidence* includes framing a sufficiently strong *I*, being able to make judgments, and having an undistorted sense of reality. In the mature adult, self esteem and self-confidence are joined in the capacity for *empathy*, knowing what others are experiencing without making it one's own experience. Failure to provide these gifts causes the child injury that slows or stops the maturing process (narcissistic injury). It also triggers the development of a defensive structure that distorts a child's perception and that generates a damaged and self-focused adult.

NARCISSISM AND SEPARATION

At birth, children are pure narcissists. This initial state of egocentricity is called *primary narcissism*. The self is perceived as connected to all things. Infants are not the center of their universe, they *are* the universe. Nothing beyond them exists that is not themselves.

Sigmund Freud's pioneering work identified the stage of primary narcissism and other stages in the developmental process, which has become the beginning point for all later work. All major theoreticians agree that primary narcissism is the first developmental stage. Here the infant wants only to be satisfied. Infants are hungry and are fed. They cry and are picked up. They are uncomfortable and they have their diapers changed. They are soothed and held, and it feels good to them. This stage may last for some time.

17

Beginning with Freud, most theoreticians have considered narcissism to be a normal stage of infancy. During this first stage, the child is building the ego and searches for a mirror self. In normal development, the infant transfers this infantile pleasure drive to others. Heinz Kohut (1971) refers to this maturing self love found in all normal adults as normal self-esteem. Freud was convinced that the ability to love both others and the self serves as a protection against becoming ill. Forming a series of identifications or connections with loved objects (other persons) is primarily a subjective process. We make of it what we perceive it to be more than what it is (Duruz 1981).

No consensus exists, however, concerning the theoretical goal of the infant drive. Freudians understand it as a drive for pleasure, and the British Object Relations school, a drive for connectedness. Both contain truth. The consensus is that energy is expended by the infant toward something, either love or pleasure. Whatever is the goal of the drive and how successful or satisfying its outcome determine whether the next stage of development happens in a healthy or an unhealthy way.

Analytic thought agrees that narcissism is a normal developmental stage out of which children grow after six to eighteen months, but before thirty-six months of age. Narcissism is a stage during which no distinction between *self* and *other* is available.

After about six months, infants begin to know themselves to be separate from others. This process unfolds over the next twenty-four to thirty months and becomes the primary task of each human being pursuing emotional maturity. If a child does not move beyond this stage of primary narcissism, then the result is abnormal or *pathological narcissism*—a chronic condition of incomplete early development. This basic condition manifests itself in a variety of ways.

Margaret Mahler is credited with taking Freud's concept of separation and raising it to a key developmental level. Mahler asserted that at about eighteen months of age, the child begins the process of separating from mother or begins to perceive itself as a separate individual. Both Melanie Klein and Mahler believe that symbiotic connection with mother is necessary for normal development. Should the mother not provide adequate nourishment or nurturing, the self becomes damaged because separating from someone to whom one never was initially joined is not possible. Neither is it possible to join without first being separate.

Klein examined early infant processes in terms of love, hate, and the fluctuations between them. She believed that for the child, an understanding of relationships begins at the mother's breast. The presence of the breast brings gratitude, while the absence of the breast when needed is experienced as a willful, aggressive act by a sadistic other. Klein says that gratifying experiences with the mother and identification with others who are perceived as good are key to healthy development.

The task of separation, which begins at about the age of eighteen months, is the primary developmental task for all individuals. This task works or does not work depending on the emotional condition of the parents. If separation occurs, then there is health. If it does not, then difficulties begin. An incomplete separation process and the defensive structure that results from it set the stage for the first half of adult life. From that point onward, defenses often begin to break down as life grows increasingly complex. If events become complicated or traumatic enough to overcome the limits of the defenses, then this may happen even before mid-life.

TWO GIFTS FROM PARENTS

At our birth we have all of the emotional, physical, and intellectual equipment we need in order to mature. Our intelligence, our physique, our body's chemistry, and other things have been genetically transmitted. The ways in which we develop cognitively are also built in.

But we cannot mature alone. Only very few members of the animal kingdom can survive alone at birth, and we are not among them. The more complex the creature, the less able it is to survive by itself. And so we come to parents and parenting—our parents from whom we need two gifts. What they provide interacts with our relatively unformed selves and our built-in equipment to set the stage for a large portion, if not all, of the rest of our lives.

Kohut's understanding of human development is more positive and hopeful than that of his predecessors. In Kohut's work the same components—child and the parents—are present. Unlike Freud, however, Kohut believes that from birth the child is instinctively driven toward wholeness, health, and maturity. Kohut changed the language and framework of human development from a description of a kind of life sentence established by maternal deficit, attention in surplus, or abusive distortion into a process whereby the wounded can be helped over time to put away their distortions and live their lives in richer ways. But during most of their childhood and adolescent years and much of their adult life, damaged children perceive themselves as "too good," "too bad," "too different," or "too unique" to be helped by a merely mortal psychotherapist. In Kohut's model parents are needed to give the child the simple gifts it deserves: a love and respect for the self, and a realistic perception of the world.

Like Freud, Kohut believes that the newborn child cannot distinguish psychologically between itself and other persons or things around it. With adequate parenting, the child moves to a more separated or cohesive stage of development. Kohut's theory of child development has its roots in Freud, Mahler, and Klein. In extending their work, he observed that unless the separation process is complete, the child will grow up seeing other people only as extensions of itself. This insular perception becomes part of the defensive posture of the wounded. Because they have never completed their own separations, they cannot relate to genuine others, but only to "others" perceived as extensions of themselves. This creates the illusion of control and supports the fantasy that there will be no additional emotional hurt or pain.

In order for the instinctual drive toward wholeness and maturity to be maintained, parents need to support a child's drive to have a sense of self-worth. They should also offer strong support and paint a realistic picture of the world. Both parents play critical roles in healthy emotional development. Neither mother nor father dominates.

Self-Confidence—Adaptation to the Real World

Self-confidence (internalized idealized parent) is a truthfulness that the world is a place to be lived in and influenced by us and a realistic awareness that this world is simultaneously safe and dangerous. In so-called traditional families, fathers are viewed as changing and responding to the world, but mothers, too, are increasingly making their mark. In many African American families, the mother has been a self-confident model responding to the world for her children for many years. The presence of a father or a strong and confident male, however, is still key to the developmental process. A 1991 film, *Boyz 'N' the Hood*, makes this point strongly. Children need a living ideal toward which to aim, and this ideal is a true gift when presented well. Internalized self-confidence goes beyond the ideal to an accurate perception of reality that is neither unduly pessimistic nor optimistic.

Self-Esteem—The Apple of My Own Eye

Mother is often the person with whom the infant's first major interaction takes place. As the infant makes its first partial separation from the mother, it begins to shift consciousness from being the whole universe to being just the person in the center of it. And so comes the first jolt of reality.

The very young child, still unable to distinguish between herself and the rest of the environment, or to see herself as part of a greater whole, has an exaggerated sense of self. To a young child, the world consists of the child alone. The experience of defining the world solely in terms of self is called *the grandiose self* (Kohut 1971).

In early interaction the parent holds the child, feeds the child, and talks to the child. The parent cradles the child at middle distance, looks into the small face, and smiles. The parent looks into the infant's eyes. The child responds to the noise, the warmth, the feeding. In the eyes of the parent, the child sees a reflection of itself. This interaction begins to introduce the notion of an "other" and so tames the child's initial grandiosity. As separation continues, additional grandiosity gradually gives way, taking with it the internalized notion that the child is totally self-accepting and self-adoring, a notion originating with the parent's reflected acceptance of the child. Children internalize the image of a loved self and convert it to self-esteem. The internalized reflection, "becomes instinctual fuel for our . . . ambitions and purposes, for the enjoyment of our activities, and for important aspects of self-esteem" (Kohut 1971).

Confident Esteem—The Need to Idealize

A child needs a parent to idealize, to put on a pedestal and admire deeply. Gradually, as we watch what we admire, our ideal becomes internalized. We are helped by our ability to internalize as we organize the world in which we live and respond to it appropriately. As adults, the idealized parent, now internalized and separated from the real parent, serves as guide. In an evolutionary fashion, what began with a real parent becomes our "ideal."

Whether or not a parent is worthy of being thought ideal is not the issue. Examples abound indicating that a child idealizes one parent or both regardless of their character or even their behavior. Children with alcoholic fathers often idealize them and feel sorry for their failure to adjust to a cruel and unjust world. The children of violent parents are much more likely to have violent urges than children from other homes. This seems to suggest that some bizarre form of idealization has been internalized and later manifested as a distorted notion of how life ought to be.

More often only one parent is idealized. For children, only one other can be held as highest. Idealizing both parents equally is difficult because the idealizing process has a singlemindedness about it.

If we reflect on our own personal experience, then we ought to be able to find evidence of having idealized one of our parents, or aspects of them both, and of having made that ideal internal to us. No matter how hard I resist, I am aware, with advancing age, that an internalized mother and father continue to live on in me. A former assistant in a mental health project once commented that her publicly presented *joie de vivre* was simply the terror that she would become like her mother. She is still terrified, if her seemingly youthful enthusiasm can be used as an indicator.

The primary role related to self-esteem is most often played by the mother. Does this mean that the primary role in the development of self-confidence is played by the father? Not necessarily. One cannot even say with certainty that the idealized parent image will come from the parent of the same sex as the child, although the same-sex parent will exercise a powerful influence in the child's development.

What is the importance for males of the role played by the father? My own research sought to uncover some of the differences between successful and less successful male clergy by studying 150 male clergy who had been ordained for between fifteen and twenty-five years. The single most important factor in distinguishing between those clergy who were successful in their careers and those who were less so was their relationship with their fathers. Those clergy who were successful reported close and present relationships with their fathers, whereas those who were less so did not. It appears that, at least in this case, male clergy are likely to have more successful careers if their fathers were present in their lives to serve as an ideal and model as they tested reality.

What about fathers and daughters? A New York researcher conducted a study of ballerinas. She wanted to know what made the difference between ballerinas, a career involving both personal display and aesthetic sensitivity and women in other careers requiring less drive. Kohut provided the developmental base for her research, which suggested that permission-giving fathers are a necessary component for those professions requiring the regular demonstration of competence before an audience. A study of ballerinas raises an interesting question regarding a religious profession as a career involving public display and aesthetic sensitivity. Successful women as well as men are both more likely to be healthy and paradoxically more dysfunctional than those in other careers. Career choice seems less a function of skill than the ability to demonstrate publicly that skill; this ability is a product of parenting (Hamilton 1989). A 1991 study further supports the notion that both health and dysfunction in empathic function exist in greater proportion among female dancers than in the population as a whole (Kalliopuska 1991).

The determiner of self-confidence has been the mother in many cases. But research evidence for this judgment is muddy. In contrast, two studies make the father's role important for healthy development.

Regardless of sex, the idealized parent strongly influences the child concerning the world and how to make one's way in it. This promotes *self-confidence*—a confidence that the observed is the real, and that this seen reality opens possibilities for action. Self-confidence is knowing that there are people to relate to and that no matter how hard one works, or how much one cares, we will still get hurt and still recover from it. It is trusting that we will find pleasure and that we will die. It is also knowing that in between birth and death, things may be interesting.

The vision of reality that fosters self-confidence will not apply in extraordinary times when events such as the Holocaust, the purges under Stalin, or the persecution of Native Americans in nineteenth-century America are present. Certain groups will also find a positive view of reality impossible—for example, Ethiopian peasants, the majority of African Americans in cities, Native Americans today, the American homeless, or many minority populations of different times and places. The realities experienced by these people are quite different but no less real. Self-confidence is a sacrifice to realistic perception of tragedy.

With daunting universal sameness, the interaction between parents and children, seemingly well designed to achieve maturity, nonetheless goes terribly awry generation after generation. The parents' own woundedness, passed on in some form to the child, becomes the predominant influence in the process. As the child, in its growth, both seeks and fears freedom, the parents' choices collide with the growth and block the necessary emergence of a tolerance for ambivalence.

2

WOUNDS AND DEFENSIVE
STRUCTURES

People more readily attribute their dissatisfactions to recent events than to long-ago developmental damage. When they seek counseling, therefore, they imagine that solving these immediate problems will improve their whole life. Some people ask for more time together, better communication, more money, more time away from work, more support and appreciation from superiors, spouses, or children, a different job, more frequent sexual intercourse, less sexual pressure, a little more something, or a little less something. Some other people imagine that their lives will be more satisfying if certain other persons would change or simply disappear.

But current problems are almost always rooted in our wounded condition and the ways in which we have structured ourselves to compensate. Our dissatisfactions with life or career fit into the total context of our selves. As our contexts expand and our lives become more complex, we become more likely to blame other people or external events for our difficulties. The pressures of the present deplete the energy we could expend on looking backward. We chip away at current intrusions of early damage, hoping to improve the feel of the whole. Everything seems simpler this way, and our multilayered lives, in which past and present intermingle, seem clearer.

The strategy does not work. When we become aware that our lives, loves, fantasies, careers, and beliefs have been heavily influenced by early wounding, several failures may already have been added to the trash heap of our past. This cannot be changed; it is done.

The damage originates with parenting, but the responsibility for continuing the process cannot be assigned to damage inflicted by parents long ago. The individual's resistance to maturing and an accompanying fear of adulthood become so great for some that they come to mistake their own immaturity for maturity. The result of their resistance is a kind of perennial emotional childhood.

WOUNDEDNESS AND DISTORTION

Woundedness may be defined as the inability to mature. In a wounded person, the instinctive drive is blocked or inhibited. This damage is internalized by the child, so that it is now a part of the child instead of outside. The self of this damaged child cannot form into a cohesive whole. Instead, it remains fragmented, with some parts available consciously and other parts hidden and beyond the reach of consciousness. The damaged adult lives a life motivated or driven by hidden and still childlike parts.

At the beginning of the twentieth century, ideas related to emotional maturing were considered pioneering and radical. Now they are accepted. What parent has not believed or privately feared that whatever goes wrong in their children's lives has its roots in something they did or did not do as a parent?

No one succeeds in growing up unscathed. All of us are wounded in different degrees. Maturing, then, requires moving through the woundedness. We live in this condition like aging children in the half-light of life's possibilities. This woundedness promotes distortion, and all of us distort to some degree—it is the human condition. The existence of distortion alone does not put us at risk. Rather the degree of distortion, not its presence, creates the at-risk condition.

At one extreme, some parents treat their children with such dependent adoration that the children are made to feel that they are not only the apple, but the super-apple of their parents' eye. This makes such children think of themselves as superior, unique, and not like the rest of the poor apples in the universe. These super-apples believe they are not measured by the same criteria as others. At another extreme, many parents communicate only conditional acceptance. This conditional apple-ness is perhaps the most common. Children come to know that they are the apple only under certain conditions. Still another extreme occurs too frequently: Some parents communicate to the child that only the parent is at the center and that any performance or attribute of the child reflects on the parent, positively or negatively. Each success is the parent's success, and each failure occurs only because the child did not try hard enough.

Interaction with other people, specifically with a parent, gives us self-worth. We pay a price for it, giving up the idea of being the whole show. We have to realize that others are out there in the world; some even admire us. Paradoxically, we may be able to see these outside people as external to us only because we see them as admiring us.

Kohut (1971, 178) would refer to this phenomenon of externalizing perception in order to be able to internalize judgment as the *taming* of the grandiose self. The word *taming* when applied to human interaction sounds like something that is done with animals. Kohut's use of the word, however, is akin to the word *discipline*. Think of this baby, this self-centered and grandiose me, as becoming disciplined. At its root the word suggests "open to be taught." Look at the opposite, the undisciplined. When I am not disciplined, I act and react. I learn nothing because I believe the world exists only for my pleasure. I take and never learn. I am angry when things and others do not respond to my desires. Such is the untamed or undisciplined grandiose self.

DEFENSIVE STRUCTURES

All defenses initially begin as a response to parental injuring by which the child creates a defensive structure intended to serve two purposes: first, to shield the child from further injury by parents; and second, to protect the child from those parts of the self that are perceived as potentially harmful. But hiding parts of ourselves from our conscious self distorts our perception of others, because the others are then seen not as they are (that is, separate), but as extensions of ourselves, pieces that are deemed either dangerous or necessary.

The distortions caused by a defensive structure can be understood in the context of an actual life event, such as falling in love. Generally, this process involves a perception, usually below the level of consciousness, that another will make up for all the injury we have received in the past. After a time, however, the loved one may become perceived as dangerous, potentially hurtful, or simply disappointing or unexciting, but nothing has really changed except our perception. Our own damage has distorted our perception by projecting our selves into an other, so that we perceive the world and those in it as parts of ourselves.

Transference

When we project parts of ourselves outward, we make the world and those in it become part of us. When clergy have difficulty relating to a particular member of their congregation, a supervisor may suggest that the difficulty has something to do with problems the professional had with a parent. This is not the same as saying that the congregational member resembles the clergyperson's parent. Rather, the supervisor is suggesting that that aspect of the parent that the religious professional long ago made part of him- or herself is being thrust out again and attached to the member of the congregation. This process called *transference* gets in the way of seeing other people clearly. Narcissistic injury distorts the world for people by making them see others only as extensions of themselves.

Why do the victims of narcissistic injury refuse to look at the world without distorting it? Basically, because they are afraid that the world, if seen clearly, will continue to hurt them. They also fear that other people, if permitted their own autonomy, will threaten and even overwhelm them. Internalizing is a form of controlling by recreating in controllable form. The victim of narcissistic injury fears being left without others, but also fears being overwhelmed by relationships.

The Unconscious

The action of defenses is unconscious; thus the damaged person has no real idea that complex protective defenses like internalizing are in operation. As people mature, more and more material that once was unconscious becomes conscious. This complex of protective defenses, which together form the defensive structure, disappears from our consciousness and becomes invisible to us. This mental activity beyond the reach of consciousness is called the *unconscious*.

According to early notions, the unconscious was a sort of box, a repository of the difficult, the painful, and the unacceptable. Such a model might lead one to expect that if the box opened, a person would be on the way to health. More contemporary notions view the unconscious as a process. Freud's contribution of the concept of the unconscious, or, more accurately, his refinement of the concept, has become an accepted part of Western culture.

The unconscious, unlike conscious processes that can be brought forward by mental attention, remains in part invisible and inaccessible. The goal of analytic therapy is to make unconscious material available to the patient. While thought, language, and logic are the tools of the conscious, unconscious processes operate by a different system. Many of the thoughts and wishes of childhood, in which there is no ordinary logic, no time, and little negative judgment, are unconscious. Contradictory, unacceptable, or even violent notions can exist in the unconscious in repressed form and motivate an individual from day to day.

The Core of Being at Risk

Distorted perceptions of reality result in the individual's seeing and feeling the world differently, so that he or she responds disproportionately to motivations that originate in the unconscious and are expressed in feelings and reactions rather than in thought. The individual then reacts to the world and to others as if the distortions are the reality. The damaged religious professional lives within an emotional world of extremes or constrictions; that is, the situations encountered by such a person generate either an exaggerated emotional response or a constricted one. In effect, the at-risk person perceives distortedly and acts in terms of self-protective defenses.

For clergy the unconscious can be even more powerful after distorted perceptions of God and faith are stirred into the mix. Religious professionals claim to interpret universal mysteries to believers as well as to explain the meaning and purpose of life. They are therefore in a position to be potentially dangerous when their own perceptions are distorted.

The Range of Distortion

There is a spectrum of distortion from mild to extreme, and very few of us are in a position by ourselves to judge how much distortion will put us at risk. Freud once warned us to "beware of the wiles of our own ego" (May 1967). This suggests that how we perceive our functioning is not always to be trusted. We must also be aware of how others see us. We must face the facts and fantasies of our raising, not what we imagine we have done with it. Even though it may not be manifested in harmful ways at present, severe damage in childhood eventually puts us at risk. As indicated, narcissistic damage is an all-or-nothing process. It happened or it did not happen. The severity or degree of the damage correlates with the extent of distortion and ranges from mild to extreme.

Nor can genetics be ruled out as determinants of risk. Why do adults who were abused as children seem to respond to treatment in widely different ways? If damage is damage then there ought to be similarities in the rate and kind of response. This is not the case, however. Some adults respond better and more quickly than do others. Some never achieve health, but remain dysfunctional throughout the course of their lives. Intelligence and the ability to use it are the best but not the only predictors of success; a genetic or biological factor also appears to be involved.

Religious professionals who are at risk demonstrate different degrees of the same thing: That is, the effects of the narcissistic injury on the adult religious professional are strikingly similar, manifested in only a few ways but in a wide spectrum of severity.

DETECTION OF AT-RISK PROFESSIONALS

Clergy are most often unaware that they are at risk. Their own perceptual distortions lead them to believe that they are functioning adequately; and yet manifestations of anger or hostility, the alienation of counselees or congregational members, and the regular assigning of blame to others indicate that something is wrong. But often the religious professional will deny the presence of symptomatic behaviors, even when confronted directly.

Mainline religious communities both assume and expect that their professionals will be mentally healthy and mature. They want to support those professionals in need and at risk, but often do not know how. One might assume that similar caregiving professions, such as psychology, medicine, social work, or teaching, might require those entering the profession to manage emotionally inhibiting material before entering. This is not universally so. These professions have mechanisms for dealing with dysfunction, but only after the dysfunction is manifested. No profession insists that the individuals be whole before entering.

Despite progress by religious denominations in working with their professionals, or increased expectations that psychologists pursue wholeness as part of their training, there are presently no helping professions that universally mandate wholeness as a requirement for those in the profession and provide a satisfactory way for wholeness to be achieved. Nevertheless, the public who seek help from clergy or those in other helping professions generally expect that those they consult will be whole and mature.

While most mainline religious groups use comprehensive psychological assessments as part of their candidacy process, these assessments often use self-report rather than dynamic instrumentation. These self-report instruments are tests in which the candidates report their perceptions about themselves in response to a set of questions. Dynamic instrumentation moves beyond self-perception to underlying themes which may be beyond the candidate's awareness. A dynamic profile of a candidate helps the denomination to seek help for a candidate when necessary. Several dynamically oriented instruments measuring similar processes are necessary to paint a comprehensive picture.

The behaviors that clergy exhibit later in their careers are not always clearly visible at the beginnings, even for second-career persons. While we might wish for a magic psychological assessment process that will uncover the material lurking below the surface, psychologists' predictions about future behavior are not always accurate. A developmental history is needed in the assessment of church professionals. That history can help denominational leaders to determine, early in a candidate's career, the kind of help and support that he or she needs.

For example, the consequences of sexual misconduct for a religious professional are severe. But this behavior did not just appear without warning. A religious system attentive to the development of its professionals has a better than average chance of helping them to address the results of the damage they have sustained. Sexual misconduct is always related to other material in the individual's life history. It is the product of immaturity resulting from early damage. It may stem from the defensive structure or from splitting. It is better to take measures to address damage than to make excuses for misconduct later on.

Some would protest that there are fewer people interested in religious professions than before, and thus we are no longer at liberty to be choosy in selecting them. On the contrary, religious systems cannot afford *not* to be choosy. An at-risk professional may do immeasurable damage to a whole congregation. Just because a candidate looks and sounds good to some screening committee does not mean that he or she is not at risk.

CULTURAL AND GENDER-BASED INFLUENCES

Cultural influences have profound effects on the development and expectations of the caregiving professional. Therapists, along with almost everyone else, often use cultural norms as a gauge of normalcy. Persons raised in Christian environments view the world differently than do persons raised in Jewish homes. African Americans view the world differently than do Asian Americans.

If racism, sexism, or creedism is a cultural norm, then those who are not racist, sexist, or credal traditionalists are the marginalized of the culture. When enough such persons challenge the norm, then a new understanding of normalcy may emerge. Not long ago, to be normal in Washington, D.C. meant going through a "Whites Only" entrance to the movies and drinking from a "Whites Only" fountain. Now a whole generation of people has grown up who have not had that experience of legalized segregation. Does this mean that there is less racism on the planet? Probably not. Norms such as racism can be firmly fixed within our psyches by means of familial nurture.

Gender provides another powerful cultural difference. To paraphrase noted sex researcher Harry Benjamin (1966, 7), a deciding factor in our future identity begins with the quick look by the obstetrician or the midwife and the declaration that "it's a girl," or "it's a boy." Other characteristics further complicate the picture. African American women complain that white women want to apply their white standards of normalcy on the black community. That is not possible. An African American woman is different from a white woman and operates by different cultural norms.

Not long ago, an emotional condition called *neurasthenia* was as common a diagnosis as depression is today. Now it has virtually disappeared from use. Its symptoms were a general nervousness with physical symptoms as diverse as fatigue, dizziness, irritability, diverse physical pains, fears, and anxiety. It was thought to have its origins in the sexual repression of the day and was believed to be a sort of nervous exhaustion. The gender-specific treatment was telling. If a man was diagnosed with the condition, he was encouraged to increase his activity. It is postulated that the origin of Teddy Roosevelt's Rough Riders lay in Roosevelt's having been diagnosed as neurasthenic. If, in contrast, a woman was diagnosed with the condition, the medical advice and proposed cure was bed rest. While we have come a long way since neurasthenia, there is yet strong evidence that men and women are treated differently by medical professionals and by the society as a whole. One need only compare the amount of money spent on research for breast cancer with the amount invested in prostrate-cancer research to see the continuing difference.

Today, the incidence of depression is widespread with almost twice as many women as men experiencing the symptoms and receiving the diagnosis (*DSM III-R*, 231). I have suspected for some time that what is called depression in many women is actually oppression or repression. Women tend to be on the losing end of tradeoffs and to assume they need to tolerate far more in relationships than is reasonable, and they are too often prone to denial.

Religious communities, more than other types, claim to use justice as their standard. Nevertheless, some churches continue to refuse ordination to women as well as to homosexuals, and on a global scale sexism continues rampant in the religious professions. Sexism, of course, reflects the continuing impact of the general culture upon the churches. Interactional friction between the growing churches of Eastern Europe and the Third World on the one hand, and the somewhat stagnant American churches on the other, is exacerbated by this gender-based issue.

What about American women and men? At a training event that I attended several years ago men were put into one group and women into another. The men spoke easily with one another, but the conversation was shallow. This seemed to reflect both the continuing presence of the "old boys' club" and a male's conditioned inability to discuss emotional material (though a small emerging men's movement does seem to be making some changes).

Women at the training event reacted differently from the men. They formed not one large group but several smaller groups. No immediate sisterhood emerged in the total group, although in some circles, including academic, there is a new sisterhood emerging. There does not yet appear to be one in the religious community.

Several paradoxes are involved. Women value traditionally feminine characteristics in men, such as tenderness, nurturing, warmth, and caring. These are characteristics often found in male religious professionals. Women also value traditionally male characteristics in other women such as aggressiveness, certainty in decision and goal, and forthrightness. Women seem not to value traditionally feminine characteristics in other women and do not value stereotypical male characteristics in men.

What do men value in themselves? Most continue in a stereotypical male path. Increasingly, however, men value the softer and less macho. This is not true in all American cultures, however. What do men value in women? Unfortunately, expectations remain strongly traditional even among the ranks of professionals, including clergy.

Even the most enlightened parents raise girls differently from boys. Lyn Mikel Brown and Carol Gilligan's recent research at Harvard (1992) followed a group of girls in a private New England school from age ten until age sixteen. Their results indicated that at about age eleven these girls believed that they could do anything they set their minds to. They were clear about this and were able to begin to set goals to accomplish their objectives. These same young women by age fifteen had lost their certainty. They no longer believed that they could do or be what they wanted to. They had already begun to be affected by the cultural limitations placed on them as women.

One gender-specific phenomenon seems to be related to physical or sexual abuse of children by parents. In cases where a parent substitutes a relationship with a daughter for a relationship with a spouse perceived to be bad, these triangulated relationships tend to produce adult women who are victims. In cases where a father or mother substitutes a son for the spouse, that son is more often an abuser as an adult. Here we have an example of the same damage generating different results but setting the stage for a repetition of the abuser/victim drama of the preceding generation. It takes one abuser and one victim for a tragedy. As many more men than women are abusers and many more women than men are victims, the story of abuse and victimization is often repeated.

Freud made the oft-discussed remark that anatomy is destiny. In a sense it is true. When women carry a life and bear children, and form an early attachment to them via breastfeeding, they obtain power. Throughout their work, Melanie Klein, Anna Freud, and Margaret Mahler strongly reinforced the point that women's attachment shapes the life of the child in ways unavailable to men. There is good evidence that women conceptualize and value things differently than men do. With one exception, there is no evidence to suggest that men and women are unequal in capacity. Social psychologists agree that there are no intellectual differences between the sexes. There are, however, physical performance differences with men being stronger and women having greater endurance. The one major difference is in aggression—male aggression is a biologically based gender difference. There is even a strong finding that males tend to be more aggressive than females. Little wonder that the male-dominated planet has seen so much violence.

Is the difference in nature or do cultural nurturing differences account for the majority of differences? The jury is not only still out but will probably find answers in a manner consistent with the times as much as with the facts. It has always amazed me to see how the categories, the criteria, and the mood of a culture determine what it discovers to be "true."

Ultimately both sexes need the same thing for mature development: self-esteem and a perception of reality. If parents give boys the sense that they can do and become many things that girls cannot, they have given them a culturally distorted view.

THE PARENTS' LEGACY

Psychologies, like philosophies and theologies, are only limited ways of looking at the whole. No single discipline or viewpoint will do full justice to reality. One needs to be open to change and to know that rigidity of any sort distorts.

The sum total of reality is never fixed in any one moment. Reality has a fluidity or process about it. This is one reason why it is so difficult to be precise in defining self-confidence. Indeed, self-confidence is most easy to define when it is seen in context, meaning the particular circumstances in which an individual finds identity and a sense of worth within reality. What, then, do we mean by reality? We can talk about a range of reality, a flexible range, but one that has outside limits.

What places some people outside the normal range of reality? There are many factors including genetics or physical trauma, but, again, one of them is parents who damage their children. Parents can witness to their children that the world is filled with people who are not trustworthy and are waiting to take advantage of them. Parents can be overprotective and never let their children cross the street alone even after they are adults. Parents can give false assurance that everything will be all right when their own lives show otherwise. In subtle ways they can suggest that they are not much concerned about or involved in the life of the child. All these messages offer a distorted world to children.

How do I know that what I am seeing in others is a distortion? Not because it is different from my own experience, but because it is beyond the range of what might be called a mature response. I know also that more flexible and dynamic approaches to reality are preferable to more rigid perceptions.

Theories of self-psychology fly in the face of those people who would withhold affection from a child in order to teach the child to "act grown up" and "stop being spoiled." It is essential to healthy growth for the internalized reflection of the parent to become a part of normal undamaged functioning (Kohut 1971).

While the role of fostering self-esteem in the child is most often played by the mother in traditional family structures, it is not exclusively a female role. It makes sense, however, that biological factors make the mother a key person. Breastfeeding, like pregnancy and childbearing, is biologically determined, and breastfeeding offers human beings their first experience of being cared for or accorded acceptance.

Historically, mothers have played the role of fostering self-esteem more than fathers. Despite current increased consciousness of sex roles, this task still falls to women, even in "enlightened" households. Recent studies on the division of parenting and housework tasks indicate that men have improved in their assumption of responsibility, but the percentage of increase has only risen from 11 percent to 20 percent. Women continue to assume the major share of the responsibility of parenting and housework.

In divorce, the mother most often maintains custody of the children and is therefore a central influence. The younger the children of a divorced couple, the more likely is the father to disappear gradually as an influence. Some recent studies have raised the hopeful possibility that in some cases of divorce the grandparents of very young children are perhaps as important as parents. Some recent evidence suggests that we are returning to a three-generation household like that of the last century. It has possibilities but also problems.

Does it make a difference whether the mother or the father takes the role of granting self-acceptance? Probably not. It is only necessary for the role to be carried out effectively. It may even be most desirable for the role to be shared.

DEVELOPMENT OF EMPATHY

When the two essential gifts of self-acceptance and a sense of reality are adequately conferred, the child is enabled to continue an uninterrupted journey toward maturity. Self-acceptance and a sense of reality make the child capable of empathy. The empathic life is a responsible and responding life in which impulses can be controlled, relationships can be established and maintained, ambivalence is tolerated, the full range of emotions is experienced, and reflection or disengagement becomes as much a part of the life process as action or engagement.

Empathy is different from sympathy, but the words are at times confused and used as synonyms. The difference is important.

Empathy and love are probably closer to each other in meaning than are empathy and sympathy. Empathy has its roots in the Greek word *empatheia*, meaning passion. Empathy is an emotional and passionate encounter with others and with the environment. It is not sexual, but it is sensual in the best sense of that word. An empathic person is able to identify with and understand another's situation or emotions. This person knows what the other is feeling without internalizing those feelings.

Sympathy is more akin to affinity. When there is affinity between people, what affects one person affects the other. In a sense the two people are not two but one. Hence we have the Italian term simpatico—meaning together, one. The root of this term suggests a process in which the feelings of one spill into the life of another. There is no separation.

Empathy, along with self-esteem, is another measure of maturity (Kohut, 1971). Self-esteem and self-confidence together make empathy possible. The combination of self-esteem and self-confidence is the greatest gift parents can give a child. It enables the child to know what another feels without misinterpreting or internalizing—that is, a child can know how another feels without needing to "fix" the other, make the "bad feelings" go away, or assume unnecessary responsibility. An assumption of responsibility may be appropriate, however, if the situation has been created by the child.

Empathy happens naturally when one has good self-esteem and self-confidence. One becomes able to empathize because one has had the experience of being empathized with during the critical formative years.

The empathic child knows what emotional stuff is his or hers and what belongs to others. There is a clear sense of a boundary. A mature person knows where he or she begins and ends and where another person begins and ends without needing a spillway between the two. A sense of boundaries grows out of the healthy separation that comes with adequate parenting. Intimacy with another is possible only when one has a clear sense of the self as separate and adequate. A confident self-perception will correctly place the self in a context among others.

The gifts of self-esteem and self-confidence are necessary for the journey to adulthood, and each child has a right to them. Without these gifts the child is wounded and the drive to mature is repressed. Maturity is postponed (sometimes for a lifetime), emotions are either felt in extremes or inhibited, and vulnerability is increased. The child is prevented from living fully throughout a lifetime and comes to perceive persons and events in unrealistic ways.

Why are the gifts of self-esteem and self-confidence not given more often? Why do so many of us come to recognize that all is not well in our own lives, only to have to witness it all over again in our children? Why are all the ways available to alter our life's course so difficult?

The answers to these questions may be considerably more simple than the giving of parental gifts. It is almost always the wounds of the parents themselves, and of their parents before them, that complicate the parent-child interaction. For parents and for the aging children they raise, the wounds are deep and generally unresponsive to casual attempts to address them.

The optimistic model of self-psychology remains incredibly difficult to accomplish. The parenting process is always a fragile and delicate one. Wounding and being wounded is not the exception but the norm.

LIVING BETWEEN
THE EXTREMES

Where we place ourselves and how much we know about the place we occupy determines how we live. In one sense we all live between extremes. Some of us swing from one extreme to the other, craving excitement and finding it only near the edges; others of us hold so close to the middle we become afraid to stir about at all. Whether we find ourselves in one of these positions or some other position on the continuum is determined in large part by what happened to us when we were young, how we were damaged, and what pieces of our self we still have not managed to locate.

All of us seek the completion of our incompleteness. We believe that one more thing, one more person, one more degree, a different career, or a different place will make us complete, and that once the missing pieces of our life are found, then our woundedness will be of no further consequence.

Some common strategies are used when chasing completeness, because just as woundedness is something we share, so, too, do methods of compensating for it resemble one another. When we believe we are on the track of a missing piece of ourselves, we tend to react in a magical or mystical way. We pursue our goal with the fervor of knights searching for the Holy Grail. Following are a few of the methods we use.

OFF TO FIND THE WIZARD

Sometimes we ascribe near personhood to what is missing from us. This can take several forms, including looking for an actual person who will complete us by directing us, and taking on what we perceive to be the wisdom represented by such a person or that person's tradition. In magical terms, the first is the search for the wizard; the second, the search for wizardry. Sometimes the two types of search go together. In religious terms, the first is as old as the hope for the messiah, and the second, as old as scripture or myths of origin.

Sheldon Kopp's book uses a Zen saying for the title: *If You Meet the Buddha on the Road, Kill Him* (1972). The clear meaning is that if you encounter anyone whom you perceive to be greater than yourself, then you are demeaning yourself in some way. Through the centuries many have been willing to follow a person, a perceived truth, or a combination of both in exchange for an end to the overwhelming sense of incompleteness.

Such quests under a religious guise are perennial. The vogue at one time was to go to India in search of a guru. More recently, New Age movements have beckoned followers to adopt a more disparate conglomeration of sources. Through the centuries forms of fundamentalism have promised answers in return for obedience. But quests are not restricted to a religious context. The search for the wizard and for wizardry occurs in bookstores and universities. For example, a well-known "self-help" author told me once that his business was selling hope. More than a few academics have taken degrees and then teaching positions in the belief that automatic wizardry would be conferred on them with the hood and the chair. Even this last decade before the millennium is prone to a heightened sense of the magic. For the religious professional, then, the search for completeness may take either a religious or a magical form. Like the pilgrim and the academic, so, too, can the religious professional wish either to see or to be the wizard.

What prompts the religious professional to undertake such a quest? The decision to identify with the church often has deep roots in painful and unresolved material from childhood. The church has long offered both wizards and wizardry, either by providing shelter from the terrors of life's extremes or by promising completion for the incomplete. To those seeking shelter a messiah is offered who sets forth a faith, which is actually a set of expectations that can function like a map. To those seeking completion—that is, authority to support their own extremes—a religious system offers protective and defining clothing: a collar and an alb. Both the protective cloak and the role of penultimate authority appear to complete these people and resolve their personal problems.

After a while, however, the cloak may fray a bit and the leader may be harder to hear. Then a kind of chronic anxiety sets in. When religious professionals refuse to recognize that personal change is called for, they usually either turn outward, blaming others for a failure that is perceived as coming from these others in the religious system, or they turn inward in depression. Sometimes clergy look to palliative and short-term relief, only to find that it doesn't do the job, or they go back to a time when they thought they were happy and safe, such as childhood or youth. They would do better to look ahead to greater maturity. Whatever strategy is taken—and this is usually determined by the degree and type of damage received—they will find that a tremendous amount of energy goes into maintaining the chosen course. Just as a country under perpetual siege, or feeling itself to be so, spends all its resources on defense, so an individual devotes virtually everything to maintaining the status quo.

Persons who are stuck in this defensive life seldom think of themselves as needing to change. They want others to change, things to change, and circumstances to change. They believe that change in others or in circumstances alone will make them be better or feel better, while actually the only certain change is the change we address in ourselves.

THE DEFENSIVE POSTURE

The development of a defensive posture early in life can hinder the maturing process, so that adult life becomes an extended form of adolescence, chosen to avoid a confrontation with the real world.

The defensive posture is a kind of protective structure adopted by individuals to fulfill three purposes. First, it protects the self from its own known undesired parts. Second, it hides those parts of ourselves we do not want to see. Third, it protects the self from perceiving hurt from the outside. One of the common effects of defensive postures is the development of a profound split between the internal and the external person. In mature people the internal and the external work together to make one integrated whole person. Not so in defensive people—they are only partial people, split within.

The resulting distortion creates people who masquerade as rational adults while they cover over a volatile, angry, confused, and frightened core of themselves. Every now and then the core peeks through the mask. This may be seen, for example, in a person's likes and dislikes, choice of job, choice of marriage partner, working style, or parenting behavior. Most of the important things that we do, whether we are mature or immature, are driven by this emotional core and not by our reason.

The defensive posture is an ancient concept, described in myth and found in writings from many cultures in many ages. Indeed, psychoanalytic writing draws upon these cultural sources to describe defensive postures. The myth of Narcissus and Echo and the story of Oedipus are at the root of the concept of narcissism and of oedipal material in human development. These myths are discussed further in chapter 5.

Psychology has delineated many and various defensive postures in the general population, of which three predominate among religious and caregiving professionals. They are *narcissism* (the need to be adored and the need for external controls), *compulsivity* (the need to do something important), and *depressed/dependency* (the need to be attached to others by helping them).

All three of these postures serve to curtail and to restrict the range of emotion available to the individual. The first, the depressed/dependent posture, limits the emotions to depression and a sense of being cut off from human relationships. The second, narcissism, limits the emotions to the extremes out of a profound fear of boredom that is born of a perceived threat that nonexistence is a synonym for ordinary. The third, compulsiveness, keeps all emotional expression within the middle ground, and is generated by a fear of the loss of control or of insanity.

DEFENSE MECHANISMS

Along with defensive postures come the mechanisms that serve to enforce and implement them. These operate at varying levels of intensity and can be exercised consciously or unconsciously.

Repression

The mildest form of a common defense mechanism is *repression*. Religious professionals, like all human beings, consciously refuse to accept things they do not want to face. They delay confrontations, avoid unpleasant social circumstances, pretend they have forgotten dentist appointments, and knowingly refuse to accept, or at least delay the acceptance of, unwelcome facts or discomforting emotions. Repression leaves some residue of awareness. Repressed persons feel more internal stress as their life and work are going awry. But repressed persons can be reached more easily than people in denial. Their unconscious anxieties can be made to speak more readily even though the material manifested is most often uncomfortable.

Denial

A defensive structure involving repression is at least more manageable than one that has progressed to the second level of defense, which is denial. *Denial* is not a conscious pretending that something does not exist or does not matter, but rather the actual passing beyond consciousness of the very facts that have generated anxiety. There is no residue of awareness as there is with repression. Attaining an awareness of anxiety is essential to unlocking this defense. This anxiety sets its stage with discomfort, dissatisfaction, and pain that will permit growth.

Unlike repressed persons, persons in denial first deny the existence of past threat or fear, and then, because they cannot completely hide the fear from themselves or face these fears, they project this past threat or fear into some situation in the present and charge that situation with all the emotional impact of the past fear. If a religious professional, for example, denies past hurts or threats to safety, then present circumstances, however minor or remote from these past hurts, will be made to carry the whole weight of this pain. The individual will vigorously and hostilely reject explanations involving the past. In true denial, the individual will counterfeit reality to maintain an alternative explanation in the present. He or she is simply not aware of the past or of its relation to the present. The past has been split off and set beyond conscious reach. Often the professional person in denial can even block off the unconsciously driven material of dreams when these tap the material being denied. Denial, then, is a defense mechanism that keeps us from knowing. Absence of awareness, or awareness denied, may be expressed physically in such maladies as muscle pain or tightness and a variety of more serious physical manifestations.

Denial is, unfortunately, common among religious professionals. It is most frequently found in the form of an intellectualizing defense. Through this mechanism cognition and emotion are completely cut off from each other, as if the professional were trying to live from the neck up. People employing an intellectualizing defense deny even the most powerful emotional material, supposing it to compromise and distort their purely intellectual understanding. They try literally to think their way through all problems, even very personal, emotional ones. The very nature of theological study abets this defense, as theology is a wonderfully convoluted academic discipline that stimulates and excites the mind. The theologian can all too easily substitute intellectual understanding for experiential understanding, even when the circumstances demand that emotions be recognized.

Uniqueness

Another defense manifestation, one most often associated with the defense posture called narcissism, and not at all unusual in religious professionals, is the assumption of personal uniqueness. Damaged children grow into adults who believe that there is no one quite like them. The intellectually inclined among these people seem largely to enter the professions, including the religious profession. Professions, in their turn, reinforce a sense of uniqueness among their members by giving them specialized training and "setting them apart" through a number of different strategies. For example, some religious groups are hierarchical, elevating clergy above laity and thus emphasizing the uniqueness of clergy. When the clergy resist mixing with laity they are sometimes actually expressing the kind of developmental damage that has sought and must maintain a sense of uniqueness. In such situations professional specialization masks interior feelings, and denial of commonality becomes a defensive denial. Within religious communities it is important to be able to determine which problems and experiences really are unique to clergy and which are somehow common to all members of a congregation.

Acting Out and Acting In

However entrenched a defensive posture has become, however great the energy used to maintain it, and however effectively it uses defensive mechanisms such as denial, repression, and a sense of uniqueness, there generally comes a point when something has to give—sometimes an explosion, and sometimes an implosion. *Explosion*, or acting out, is most often associated with the posture of narcissism, whereas *implosion*, or acting in, is more often found among depressed or dependent people or some forms of compulsives. Acting out may take the form of sexual inappropriateness, abuse, or violence. Acting in most often manifests itself in depression, commonly labeled burnout. Both are responses to the same damage.

Acting out and acting in are forms of response to the breakdown of defenses. Each is a sign that the defenses are disintegrating or temporarily unable to be maintained and that immature, primitive, and infantile impulses can no longer be contained. The person's energy is no longer sufficient to keep unconscious forces at bay. Acting out is an unconsciously driven declaration that the individual is unable to contain him- or herself. Acting in is a declaration of surrender: "I can't do it anymore!" Church professionals originally diagnosed as suffering from burnout often also manifest symptoms of acting out and benefit from an extensive reconstructive program of analytically oriented psychotherapy.

As the terms imply, acting out takes the form of relieving anxiety by outward action with or onto others, while acting in internalizes the anxiety in self-punishing ways. The former blames the world, the latter blames the self. The circumstances that precipitate the acting out or acting in are often nothing more than an increasing inability to respond to and function in the complexity and stress of day-to-day life. Whereas identifiable events or actions may have triggered the response, they often are the proverbial final straws that add to the weight of that which has already been carried and increased over a virtual lifetime. Finally and inexorably the load has become too heavy.

The behaviors that prevent acting out or acting in can be observed over the years. Indeed, they serve the function of postponing the disintegration. Depressed people, who blame themselves, work all the harder while becoming more and more depressed. This cycle of self-blame and increased labor may work for years until such people can no longer maintain the energy level and a depression immobilizes them. Narcissists who change jobs whenever they become bored by sameness are often successful until they grow older. Then they are confronted by the fact that the same requirements must inevitably be met over and over again in any career.

The defensive reactions that either stave off overt acting in or acting out or give warning of them manifest themselves on a scale from subtle to blatant. They may go unnoticed for many years and often are judged by peers to be positive and to deserve reward. Acting out can be rewarded as creativity, eccentricity, or a mark of individuality. Acting in can be celebrated as attention to detail, effective problem-solving, or hard work. While these are the marks of success in professional functioning, they may also be clues to dysfunction.

Acting out or acting in is what human beings do in order to alleviate anxiety. For example, some religious professionals describe themselves as unable to relax. They feel as if they are always waiting for something: the next telephone call, the afternoon mail, or the next committee meeting. While they blame themselves for their anxiety and know they need to relax, they often begin to work at relaxing. This only leaves them anxious about an inability to be relaxed about relaxation. If these professionals carry their own anxiety long enough, they will eventually become depressed. Chronic worrying is a form of acting in.

Other professionals relieve anxiety by spilling over emotionally or doing something that produces quick relief from anxiety. The belief that doing something relieves anxiety is a form of acting out. Clergy who are angry and blaming at home, or who throw temper tantrums on the job, or who overuse sexually-loaded humor, or who breach confidentiality are acting out. Neither actors-in or actors-out are much aware of their actions. In fact, they may not even be aware of the chronic level of anxiety they are experiencing. Religious professionals, perhaps more than other people, are aware of anxiety and the dangers of acting out or acting in at some level, because they have often helped others with problems. But they must remember that it is always much easier to see problem behavior in others than in oneself.

ACTING OUT

Acting out is most often connected to some past desire or event. It is a statement about that desire expressed repeatedly in different forms, all of which have a common theme. The acting out occurs as the result of an impulse which cannot be controlled. An impulse is like a flash. It is a momentary connection to the primitive and the unconscious. An impulse has great driving force. The individual is virtually impelled to action or must exert significant energy to resist, and seldom recognizes the origins of an impulse without appropriate interpretation. As long as the acting out is rewarded or is neither scandalous or illegal it is often tolerated, though it may not be liked or appreciated, by others. In pathologically matched relationships, the acting out can go on for years.

Acting out is almost always erotic (sexual, passionate) or aggressive (angry, rage-driven) in its origins. Often sex and violence are seen to be related to male dominance and nineteenth-century Victorianism. Perhaps if one sees sex and violence as human responses to a primary drive to connect with loved others, these two can be seen as something less threatening. An appropriate response when connecting to an other in adult love or receiving nurturing is a sensual or sensate one. If one is hurt (or, the opposite, smothered by love), then anger (or its opposite, depression), is an expected response.

Religious professionals who are able to maintain control over impulses most of the time may act out in particularly stressful situations. Candidacy processes for a church profession can be particularly stressful. Candidates are often seen at their worst by candidacy committees, which may be a good thing because the religious profession by its nature includes many points of stress. If a candidate's impulse control is inadequate, it is well to discover this early. When professionals act out under stress, it may cause harm to others or to the professionals themselves.

Why are some more able than others to control impulses and inhibit acting out? There are various explanations. Some persons do not act out because they are acting in, driving their impulses in toward themselves. Others do not act out because they have turned an angry or impulsive response into its opposite—for example, a kind of sugary kindness. Still others are simply more mature and well able to control their impulses. Dysfunctional behavior is not an all-or-nothing phenomenon. We are all on a sort of sliding scale in which some, depending on their early development, are more adept at control or have fewer dysfunctional impulses than others.

Dynamic psychology and mainline theology have remarkably similar understanding regarding the nature of the human creature. Each maintains that it is not the impulses that are the problem, but the lack of control over those impulses. Quick and strong sexual attractions, angry desires, dark wishes, a desire to scream at stupidity and thoughtlessness, anger at children so powerful that we want to hit them, and desires to end relationships because they are immediately uncomfortable are part of human life. Most persons do not act on these. Not acting is impulse control.

Examples of Behaviors.   Here are some forms of acting out that commonly occur among religious professionals:

- breaching confidentiality
- chronic complaints of busyness
- changing jobs frequently
- frustration or anger when they cannot change jobs quickly enough
- overuse of sexually loaded humor
- changing schedules often because of supposedly more important demands
- focusing attention on themselves (usually in peer settings)
- name dropping
- seductive leadership function (motivating members by force of personality)
- responding angrily when others do not cooperate with them
- chronic negative judgment of others
- adoration and pursuit of those few judged to be wonderful
- calmness on the job, anger in private
- overcommitment to activities not directly related to their jobs
- rationalizations about this overcommitment
- immaculate affairs (intimate love relationships without sexual contact).

Our sexual and aggressive core operates throughout the course of professional and personal life. It is felt as passion, curiosity, and the ability to nurture. It may also involve the ability to accomplish meaningful work, to plan, to decide, and to help others do the same. Sometimes these get some of us into trouble. Sometimes sexual and aggressive drives help to create a public crisis, sometimes a crisis that is not public.

The same drives that may be expressed in acting out are manifested in other ways in which professionals relate to congregational members, clients, or other staff members. For example, there was a twenty-eight-year-old clergyman who had never resolved his issues with his father. Since he needed a father to overcome psychologically, he took as father substitute a fifty-five-year-old fellow male staff member. When he began to demean the man's intelligence by saying that he was less sharp than he had been when he was younger, he was not speaking accurately or being simply malicious but was acting out unfinished business with his own father. The older clergyman, however, took offense, feeling threatened. He may give in to his own drives to act out by patronizing the younger man as immature and inexperienced and tolerating him as a father tolerates an unruly son.

Almost every male or female religious professional who has worked with another church professional of a different gender has confronted confusing sexual dynamics. Any two people who are repeatedly alone together will develop an emotional bond. There is no evidence that exclusively female staffs have an easier time of it than male or mixed-gender staffs. We can only say that dynamics differ with gender mix. It is not a matter of age or gender but of maturity. The religious professionals who get into a crisis are simply persons who are acting out in a more visible way than many of the rest. Inadequate impulse control and acting out are exaggerated versions of things we have all experienced.

The Affair.   An affair here is defined as a sexual relationship between consenting adults who are already emotionally attached to others. Although it may not involve actual physical contact, any affair is acting out regardless of how it is explained or rationalized.

Falling in love is a great anxiety reliever. When one is in love, reality is suspended or abandoned and along with it the whole concept of the consenting adult. This is true even when the lovers believe they are in touch with reality and have examined the consequences. Although acting out provides temporary relief from chronic anxiety, it creates more difficulty than existed before. The anxiety does not go away.

Affairs can also be seen as two kinds of acting out: sexual acting out for the participants and aggressive acting out against the marriage partners. In an affair, sexual acting out is always linked with aggression or anger at another. It is a way of getting at somebody, usually a parent in the past. Unfortunately, long-ago parents are often less hurt than the present-tense actors-out they have produced.

How does an affair develop? Gradually a man or woman begins to believe that he or she deserves better than what is found in the marriage partner. The marriage partner is seen as insufficiently stimulating intellectually or as physically unattractive. In an immature relationship the couple's sex life becomes increasingly incestuous instead of becoming richer. Each partner in an immature relationship begins the marriage as both child to the self and parent to the other partner. An immature marriage, unlike other marriages, keeps people stuck in their roles and hinders their growing together. Every bump, wart, scar, and hair on the other's body becomes familiar, but there is still no change in the self as it is related to the marriage. Therefore the other partner becomes more like a brother or sister than like a loved other. Child, parent, and sibling begin to merge. This is a form of incest.

The taboo against incest, however, is an ancient one, and the threat of incest generates immense anxiety. One does not have sex with a parent or a sibling. If the roles of mate and parent or sibling are merged, then anxiety increases, and consequently the individual begins unconsciously to look for a lover who will not also be a parent or sibling. Such a person can soon be found. Religious professionals almost always find these new persons within the religious institution. The relationship begins around common interests. There are many religious professionals for whom dedication to the work of the institution and infatuation with its professional leaders merge all too easily.

The Restless Professional.   Another form of acting out is to move from one congregation to another or from one type of professional religious work to another in the belief that this is the best way to relieve anxiety. This form of acting out seldom causes public crisis, but it may nonetheless create private crises. Sometimes men and women who have chosen congregational work come to believe they have made a mistake. Current interest in a counseling profession or interim ministry may reflect personal dysfunction as much as a new form of service. *Growth and Ministry*, a study of ordained clergy and their spouses by the predecessor bodies of the Evangelical Lutheran Church in America (Division for Professional Leadership, Lutheran Church in America [1976], 1980), found an interesting correlation. Clergy who expressed interest in counseling were also disenchanted by traditional congregational work, even though they claimed that counseling skills would enrich their own work in a congregation. They may well have believed that a setting in which they exercised more control through exercise of counseling techniques might lower their anxiety and make their lives more manageable. If so, they were expressing a false hope.

Acting out comes in a variety of forms: kicking the dog, screaming at family, sleeping with congregational members, changing professions, telling bad jokes, or undermining staff members. Why do some professionals repeatedly act out? Acting out never happens in isolation and it never happens only once. It most often occurs in bouts of greater or lesser length depending upon the stress level. It is always an attempt to relieve anxiety. Sometimes it is an act of anger, sometimes one of sexual aggression, and sometimes both simultaneously.

ACTING IN

Acting in directs emotional energy inward rather than outward. Like the protective mother grouse who draws the hunter to follow her and leave her offspring alone, the person who is acting in bends angry, violent, or sexually aggressive impulses right back on the self so that they will not go loose into the world. Sometimes acting in is a do-or-die effort to maintain control, even if it destroys the person. It can occur in two ways: the overcontrolled response and the depressed response. The overcontrolled response not only defends against loss of control; it also defends against depression. Emotional energy in overcontrolled people is directed toward holding the lid on all the time in the belief that yielding to impulse and to outbursts is the equivalent of insanity. Depressed people, on the other hand, have given up all forms of response. Overcontrolled professionals become depressed when the defensive acting in can no longer be sustained. They are not aware of how their depression is covered up by control. The breakdown of control is discussed more fully in chapter 5.

Overcontrol.   The first form of acting in, *overcontrol,* involves assuming personal responsibility for anything in the world that goes wrong. Since no one can possibly bear this much responsibility, persons who act in chronically judge themselves failures. Every failure, even a small mistake, appears monumental to these people. When failure looms so large it is to be avoided at all cost. The sense of responsibility is sometimes avoided by reworking the truth into a saving fantasy. All tasks take on tremendous importance, requiring great outlays of energy, and there are few, if any, low priorities. Overcontrolled people are so hard on themselves that they become physically tense and generally nervous. They attend to the needs of others before their own, but this is done not from generosity but from fear of rejection or abandonment. Their great need for love and approval, their need to serve, and, in some cases, their indecisiveness make others angry. Such behavior is called *passive-aggressive,* throwing responsibility for anger back onto others.

Exaggerated Expectations.   The second type of acting in is a depressed one. Depressed persons generally have exaggerated expectations of others.

Depressed persons believe that life would be better if only others were different. Because their need to be cared for is exaggerated, others always disappoint them, in what they perceive to be a reenactment of their childhood disappointments. They simply and unrealistically want others to change, and this blinds them from seeing who others really are. Often they speak of some secret knowledge they have of another's true nature, which is quite different from the one presented. This is an individual manifestation of the *pairing defense* discussed in chapter 9. Depressed people, believing themselves to be helpless, feel helpless to take responsibility for their own lives. They seldom change and just feel bad most of the time. Their depression is often accompanied by physical symptoms and chronic minor illnesses.

Depression.   The classical definition of *depression,* the most severe form of acting in, is anger directed toward the self. However, this is no longer considered a complete explanation. There are at least two additional components. Depression is a defense that permits the individual, excused by sickness, to do nothing toward improvement. It is also an inward-directed action that keeps an individual from confronting the fear of helplessness in the management of life.

That depression is more prevalent in women than in men is a culturally based phenomenon. While the disparity was once explained as a biological or genetic one, it is now seen more accurately as a male explanation of a women's issue. Cultural expectations and cultural position lead women to believe that they ought to be able to tolerate more than they realistically can tolerate. This leads women to feel incapable in the face of enormous responsibility. No woman, for example, can be expected to raise unflawed children or keep a mate in a state of constant happiness. The failure lies, however, in the culture's unrealistic expectations and not with the woman's failure to perform. Men derive sexual-political benefit from keeping women in a depressed state by perpetuating unrealistic ideals and expectations. Depression leads women to judge themselves inferior and to look dependently to men. People of both sexes are driven to depression by their own unrealistic expectations coupled with cultural expectations. Depression and dependency represent a general failure to take responsibility for one's life and an exaggerated wish to be cared for by others.

Depressed acting in reflects a general sense of one's own weakness. It also triggers a cyclical process of unrealistic hope, followed by search, followed by disappointment and further loss of self-image. Depressed people often seek relationships in which they are unequal partners so that they can unconsciously maintain their sense of failure or disappointment.

Examples of Behaviors.   Here are some acting-in behaviors commonly manifested among religious professionals:

- excessive self-blame
- acceptance of responsibilities which could be delegated
- increasingly longer work hours
- perfectionism
- overcommitment to work-related activities
- high probability of acceptance of denominational requests for extra work
- periods of depression
- high tolerance of abusive or unsatisfying relationships
- excessive dependency in relationships.

Both overcontrol and depression seek to deny anger, rage, or other emotional responses, either by keeping them under tight control or by attributing them exclusively to other people while seeing oneself as their victim.

PROTECTING AGAINST FUTURE HURTS

Religious professionals, like the rest of the human race, begin their lives as children. How does this affect their future lives as adults and, later, as religious leaders? The wounds of childhood were discussed briefly in chapter 2. This chapter looks more closely at the wounding process and its various effects, including the defensive postures it imposes, but some different vocabulary is necessary in order to accomplish this.

Most children feel personally responsible for their own wounding. In other words, children believe they deserve it. The development of defensive structures permits children to live as if they deserved wounding. One common defense is to halt artificially all psychological maturing at the point of injury in order to avoid future injury. Even with therapy it often takes a long time for a child whose damage has frozen them in place psychologically to catch up with the chronological age reached since the damage was inflicted.

This chapter discusses the ways in which the child responds to wounding. Damage to self-esteem and self-confidence results in the development of a defensive structure that distorts perceptions of self, others, and the world in which the individual lives. The nature of the distortion is also influenced by gender differences and by the combinations of genders in the wounder-wounded, parent-child relationship.

The structuring of defenses initially was intended as protection from perceived injuries both severe and slight. However, the chosen defensive posture is not directly related to the type of wounding inflicted. Other factors, such as the sex of the child and the parent, are also at play.

Extreme parental damage has been much discussed in recent years. At one extreme end of the spectrum are the obviously and severely wounding parents. These parents include addicts, abusers, and those themselves severely damaged by abuse or who are mentally ill. At the other extreme are those who inflict seemingly more subtle wounds. Sometimes the casual observer would not even recognize that these parents are wounding their children. They include the overprotective, the "good hearted," and the well-intended, who out of their own distorted understandings of love hinder their children from growing into mature and separate people. Comprising the large group of parents in the middle are the developmentally damaged and wounded ones who love and accept their children conditionally or who, because they themselves have distorted views of the nature of the real world, prepare their children for a world that does not exist. Despite the many supposedly enlightened parents of this generation, perfect parenting simply does not and has never existed.

Nor can it be predicted with certainty which defensive structure will result from a specific injury. Two children may grow up developing quite different defensive structures as a result of similar damage. This can create some confusion until one recognizes that the injury alone, and not the response to it, is common to all.

The systematic construction of a defensive structure in response to wounding comprises a kind of childhood choice-making process. There are a limited number of defensive positions available to the wounded child. The child draws from a kind of common pool of possibilities, but these possibilities are more limited than we originally thought them to be. Varying intensities and combinations of these few defensive postures account for the seeming multiplicity of defensive structures. The combinations and permutations are so varied that a small number of original possibilities seems like a large number of positions. Individuals also mix defensive positions together much like the artist mixes primary colors to create a seemingly infinite variety of color and hue. The seeming complexity of the finished product belies the simplicity of the original components.

To restate simply: Each wounded child has the same goal—that is, to not be hurt anymore. To protect from further injury, the child constructs a defensive posture. The child's drive toward emotional maturity is inhibited by fear and blocked by the defensive structure and thus often becomes frozen while the body continues to grow. The seminal work in the identification of inhibited personality structures is *Neurotic Styles* (Shapiro 1965). Shapiro's identification of styles found in the general population contributed immeasurably to the understanding of the styles discussed here.

There exist only a dozen or more structural manifestations of developmental damage. Early dynamic psychology labeled these manifestations as neurotic. Now they have been grouped as character disorders, personality disorders, or developmental damage. While the new labels are less than satisfactory, each group label suggests the structures that have come together into the distorted whole. By categorizing in groups, however, one runs the danger of imposing too rigid a typology.

It is seldom helpful to view persons in rigid categories. An individual is a compendium of personality or character parts, with each part located at some point on a sliding scale from immaturity to maturity. That the scale should be a sliding one testifies to the meaning of the term *dynamic*. Dynamic implies a changing, moving flow with power and energy.

The term *disorder*, as in character or personality disorder, creates a new problem in any attempt to understand wounded people. Disorder is a term used more in psychiatry than in psychology and as a medical term reflects the medical model. Medical specialties deal with the broken and the malfunctioning. It is inaccurate to consider injured emotional development in the same category as a broken bone. The problem, then, in talking about disorder is that the term implies something static rather than dynamic and a simple rather than a complex system. It also implies a structure that has gone off track by itself instead of being derailed by others. I prefer the word *damage* to *disorder* because the term looks outside the wounded person to the source of the wounding and then back to the person again.

Character and *personality* are virtually synonymous. They both refer to the pervasive and generally consistent pattern of behaviors and responses that together comprise a whole. Character and personality are what attracts or repels us in others. It is the way we are, the way we relate and respond to others. To use the term *disorder* in discussing character implies equal dysfunction of all parts of the whole, while a character can more realistically be seen as a mixed and dynamic compendium of mature and immature responses, or better and worse functioning parts.

The term *developmental damage* is, I believe, closest to reality because it suggests a naturally maturing process (development) that has been inhibited or blocked in an individual. Developmental damage can keep parts of the personality in a regressed and immature state while letting others grow. When one is damaged, thought, feeling, attitude, and behavior are distorted in degrees and driven by material that is largely unconscious.

Defensive structures, then, block the drive to maturity. They also hide wounds like a clumsy bandage would, shutting off primitive fears and prevent us from dealing with them from the clear air of understanding. The wound remains visible to some and invisible to the self. A dozen or so defensive structures conceal even fewer primitive fears. These are fears all children share in common despite differences of gender or circumstances. What begins as a fear of further hurt is most frequently translated into fear of death or nonexistence, fear of insanity ("going crazy"), and fear of abandonment (being desolately alone). Developmentally damaged children feel personally responsible for their own wounding and live into adulthood with shame or guilt. They also seek to maintain the negative image with which the wounding parent has characterized them. For example, if an overprotective parent has, out of the parent's own need, damaged a child by overprotection and by making the child feel inadequate, alone, and in danger of abandonment, the adult child that the person grows into will continue to feel that way. Frequently, then, it takes many years for a wounded child to be able to reconnect with a chronologically older self and to continue the process of maturing. In the case of the overprotected child, the wounded adult will have to breach the block of the defensive structure, rediscover the hidden fear, and conquer it in order to recommence maturing in that area of life.

THREE DEFENSIVE STYLES

As already mentioned, the three defensive styles manifested among the ranks of religious professionals are the narcissistic defense (externalized), the depressed/dependent defense (internalized), and the compulsive defense (internalized). These three are identical to those that exist among the general professional population of our culture. The differences between other professions and clergy in this respect are differences in proportion and not in kind. To some degree, clergy and other professionals all exhibit variations upon the three themes. Theme and variations come together like a distorted composition.

More men than women adopt a narcissistic defense. This is attributable both to the way children are traditionally raised in our culture and to the fact that we continue to value male above female children. Males, consequently, are led to think of themselves as the adored ones. Although the notion of male superiority seems intellectually abhorrent to most of us, the unconscious practices to which it gives rise continue and are rampant throughout other cultures on the planet.

More women than men are depressed/dependents. Again this can be attributed to the child raising traditions of our culture with its pronounced tendency to abuse females. We have yet generations to go before changes will pervade the whole culture and alter this phenomenon. Religious communities can be at the forefront of the needed change and have already appeared to make some significant strides. However, an investigation of the culture of mainstream religious communities suggests that there is more than residual resistance to the concepts of equality.

About an equal number of men and women adopt the compulsive defense.

Defensive Styles and Religious Professionals

There are some reasons for the fact that professional people, including religious professionals, seem to adopt these three particular responses. The choice to enter a profession is not simply a matter of opportunity and financial or intellectual resources, although these are major factors. Intelligence levels among religious and other professionals most often range from above average to very superior. More than four-fifths of the general population is de facto below the average of the professional population. Clergy, more than the average person, are more driven, more motivated to achieve, and more attracted to leadership. The defenses peculiar to driven people—narcissism, depression, dependency, and compulsion—are therefore the ones found in the clergy.

The person who joins the religious or another profession has already been set apart from the population as a whole. Consequently, such a person is often hampered in his or her ability to relate to the larger population, for professionals often cannot understand others who are not as driven as themselves. Clergy, for example, may perceive less driven persons as unmotivated, sick, or in need of being changed, while corporate executives sometimes do not understand employees who do not desire promotion.

At-risk professionals believe that they are the center of their own universe and that almost everything that happens near them needs to involve them directly. Some cannot imagine that they would be unwelcome at or near the center of an event.

No religious professional is a pure narcissist, depressed/dependent or compulsive; rather, each is a mix of the three with one being dominant. Since human developmental injury is common, not surprisingly there are factors common to all three defensive adaptations. As is discussed in the Conclusion, in order for professionals to function well in their religious work, they need to redirect toward healthy use the defensive strategies that they have developed as the result of their own developmental damage.

All three types of developmental damage and the defensive structures in which they result generate exaggerated needs that real life cannot

meet. Life and events take on an all-or-nothing quality for at-risk professionals. Some damaged people have limited emotional ranges and
difficulties in relationships. All possess a sense of uniqueness in the
sense that they feel they have no real peers; thus they imagine all other
persons to be above, below, better, worse, happier, but always different
in some way.

Secondary Postures and Borderline Personalities

Two secondary defensive postures should be mentioned because they
almost always appear in combination with the three major defenses. The
first manifests itself as highly dramatic, extroverted, and flamboyant and
most often appears with the narcissistic defense. The second defensive
posture reduces or extinguishes the human conscience. People of this
group can terrify us because they do not feel the rightness or wrongness
of their actions but do what they want when they want. Persons such as
these are among the very successful self-employed, high up the ladder
in sales or management jobs, or in the ranks of criminals. They have an
advantage over the rest of us: They can walk right over us and not feel
a thing.

   In addition to the three main defensive postures, a fourth defensive
posture should be mentioned. This is the *borderline personality*, and the
degree of dysfunction is more profound than that found in any of the
other disorders or defenses. It is not a really separate entity but a backward
extension of the narcissistic personality. Until recently, this structure was
not of concern among religious professionals, but there is evidence that
some borderline personalities are functioning at relatively high levels and
are receiving endorsements from their religious communities to pursue
a clerical profession. This phenomenon may support the belief that the
quality of those persons entering religious professions is lower than it
once was because of regular declines in the size of mainstream religious
bodies and the shortage of leaders. It may also reflect a larger proportion
of borderline personalities in the general population.

PERCEPTION DISTORTIONS

Those in the religious professions who either are or perceive themselves
to be relatively functional emotionally often have difficulty understanding
the emotionally dysfunctional of any defensive strategy group. Particularly
difficult is understanding distorted or defensive thinking: The at-risk or

the dysfunctional do not just imagine reality in a different way from the way we do; they actually see and feel reality differently.

What is the distorted life like? Imagine perceiving the Tower of Pisa as vertical and all of the surroundings as tilted. For a dysfunctional individual, the one is straight and the many are askew. All of life is perceived through the lens of the original damage. Different individuals, however, deal with damage differently. The extent of one's personal resources, be they intellectual, economic, or educational, has a direct bearing on the capacity for growth and the ability to restore the motion toward maturity.

Tremendous energy is required to live a life tainted by distortion. Imagine living and trying to maneuver as if your one main point of orientation were a tilted tower you perceived as straight, while everything else appeared to be tilted. It would seem like walking perpetually on a series of inclined ramps. Often the dysfunctional directs his or her energy toward maintaining the distortion and not toward a realignment or maturing. Think how much harder those ramps would be to climb if you had to keep thinking of them as level ground whatever the evidence to the contrary. The damaged child keeps interpreting the events of life as proof that reality lies in distortion. The monsters are real, the perceived priorities are real, and the need for constriction is real. Any attempt on the part of others to point out the truth is met with anger, disbelief, or sometimes violence.

The distortions of perception, thinking, and acting continue to ensure that the damaged person remains a perennial child until the past is adequately addressed. But it is too simple to blame present dysfunctional behavior solely on wounds inflicted by parents. The distorted messages sent by the parents have long since been internalized and have become an integral part of the perennial child. The parents are no longer the enemy. They may have matured or died. Instead, it is now a long-ago mother and father living inside and inseparable from the child who are the problem. In our culture, at least, multigenerational households in small space can easily become either tyrannies or anarchies. So it is when internalized parents are made to live within us. Either internal harmony becomes cruelly distorted or there is total cacophony.

Distortion and the Religious Professional

Like other dysfunctional people, the at-risk professional is dedicated to proving that a distorted perspective is the correct one. These religious professionals live as if their distortions are reality. Their adopted defensive structure or structures conspire to maintain this distortion and continue the damaged condition. The individual imagines that life would be better if only others would change. The companion myths of the *as-if* and the *if-only* are maintained at almost any cost. They are the only way of life the at-risk clergy know.

At-risk clergy, like other developmentally damaged people, are condemned to lead lives of extremes and exaggerations or of inhibition and constriction, such as the acting out or acting in described in chapter 3. With the common defensive postures there is either very little middle or only middle. For persons living in the emotional extreme, the middle is perceived as undesirable. For the inhibited and constricted, the extremes are nonexistent.

Several things are commonly manifested by both emotionally extravagant and emotionally constricted defensive postures. Life is an all-or-nothing process. Reaction to circumstances is exaggerated. Needs become central. Drives to satisfy needs are strong. If the drive is for safety and security, the personal cost may be compromise beyond reasonable limits or even tolerance of abuse. The experience of emotion is extreme for both the externalized (aggressive or acting-out) defensive posture and the internalized (depressed or acting-in) posture. While those in the internalized posture most often experience hurt and extreme vulnerability, those in an externalized defensive posture most often experience anger. They often use anger to mask a hurt by quickly redirecting it.

Manifestations of Damage

Damage manifests itself in language. Damaged adults use phrases that suggest resignation, hyperresponsibility, or violence: "That's the way things are" (depressed/dependent); "Life is a constant struggle" (compulsive); "I killed them, wiped them out, bowled them over" (narcissistic)—these are but a few. Such phrases indicate the predominant defensive structures. A problem, however, is that perennial children characteristically mimic their fantasy of adult language and express synthetic adult thought as a mask for their own. If one listens hard enough, however, one will discover that the words and phrases chosen often are rooted in the very wound itself and suggest perception distortions.

Beyond language, woundedness manifests itself in career choices, love relationships, parenting styles, values (including religious values), ethical decisions, and stances on any issue perceived as important. The relationship between life choices and woundedness is discussed more completely in chapters 5 through 8.

Can one go through the whole of life at risk, supported by defensive structures and living in a distorted reality? It is done often and under circumstances that never sufficiently challenge the defensive structure to disintegrate. In severely damaged or dysfunctional families, several generations must grow slowly, with most members doomed to perpetual childhood until finally one of them can grasp the instinctual drive toward maturity. While a family or parents may have inflicted the wound, it is the individual who is most driven to maintain it. Most often this is accomplished by establishing a personal set of defense systems that, like those of the previous generation, keep the same distortion alive.

Our culture has an ample admixture of wounding backgrounds and received defensive systems. Our communities include fearful and sometimes violent individualists, alcoholics, abusers, the rejected and outcast of other cultures, the enslaved, the prisoners, and the refugees. American religious cultures pride themselves on giving home to the wounded, but the complexity of the needs and the limits of available resources determine an individual's potential for growth. Remember also that we are still delivering wounds as well as healing them.

Acknowledging Damage

While much happens and many years pass between the preschool years and that time during the adult years when we begin to sense that something is wrong with us, we have, by adulthood, already sought confirmation for our distorted view of the world in many people and many experiences. Most of us, from puberty on, live with a faulty experience-recording system. We remember and recall those things that confirm our distortions. What does not confirm is dismissed and often not remembered at all.

If memory cannot be trusted, how can religious professionals consciously become aware of the damage they sustained, which may be putting them at risk? Those who feel a twinge of defensiveness when this question is posed may want to look further. Those clergy who instinctively sense they may have endured damage are more fortunate than some others.

Truly mature and healthy professionals never refuse to face facts and feelings that, they may fear, others would find shameful or that are potentially shameful to themselves. They understand and accept their own weaknesses, seeing within them the strength that paradoxically may come from them. These self-conscious religious professionals also know that if they understand unconscious drives and their source in childhood wounds, and the distorted perceptions that mask the wounds, they increase their own self-knowledge. Self-knowledge not only leads to wisdom—it also leads to thoughtful governing of one's own behavior so that one may be available for other people without either threat or danger.

The best example I have seen of self-knowledge in a clergyperson based on a realistic assessment of his own drives comes from Archbishop Rembert Weakland of Milwaukee:

> Men who leave the priesthood because of loneliness are not weak. They are simply good men who have fallen in love with good women. If we are alive, we continually fall in love. You asked me once if I have ever fallen in love. Yes—at twelve, and most recently at sixty-four. I'm falling in love all the time. When I was in my forties, the women I found most attractive were usually twenty years younger. Now that's changed; age means nothing. I find intelligent women, whatever their age, extraordinarily enticing— intelligent women who are not afraid of me, who are interested in me as me, and not because I'm well known. But I am aware of when I'm falling in love. It's dangerous ever to think that all that is over with—that you won't fall in love again. I have to be on guard not to let my emotions run away, not to make excuses to see someone who has set off the spark. So far, I've done pretty well." (Wilkes 1991, 53–54)

ASSESSING ONE'S OWN DAMAGE

Human behavior is too dynamic and complex to be reduced to a simple formula or discovered through a yes-or-no type of questionnaire. There is, however, strong evidence to support the theory that positive responses to the list of things and events below may indicate past trauma that may have been put beyond the reach of consciousness. Whatever the degree of risk to which the professional may be subject, including no risk at all, it is to the advantage of every clergyperson or counselor to ask the questions and engage in a search. To do otherwise is to invite additional risk of harm to others and to self.

No professional needs be surprised to discover that there are indications of damage in the self. It is part of the human condition to have sustained some damage. In answering the questions below, do not try to give the kind of responses that you think you ought to give; be aware that it is often easy to lie to the self even when no one else will discover it. Look as candidly as possible at the possibility of damage. See how your responses may be determining your behaviors and attitudes. If you resent the implication that something may be wrong or that you are at risk, this very resentment may be evidence that something *is* wrong or that you *are* at risk. Further, if you are uncomfortably self-conscious or easily upset when responding to the statements it may be helpful to have a close friend or intimate answer the questions as they think you would have done. This feedback may be of value in getting a more unbiased picture. Simple true or false responses will suffice.

First Cluster of Issues

- A candidacy committee is suggesting that there are things that may need to be addressed. I think they are right. I am not certain what they are talking about. I believe they are a hostile group. I believe they do not like me.

- I stay in the clergy because I don't know what else to do even though the work is generally unsatisfying.

- I want to do something else but am reluctant to go back to school. I believe others are discouraging me from entering another profession.

- I have been attracted on several occasions to parishioners and fantasized a relationship with them. I have permitted this to go too far on at least one occasion.

- I am tired much of the time.

- I have gained a lot of weight since beginning professional work.

- I am working harder each succeeding year and am not certain how to slow or stop this process.

- I would rather be on the job than at home. Marriage is less satisfying than it once was.

- I fantasize about what it is like at home when I am away and am almost always let down when I arrive. This happens even when I go home for a short time. Only after a time do I settle into the routine.

- I am negative about most things. Others have told me so.

- I believe I am different from other clergy. Many of them do not work as hard as I do. Many are not as insightful as I am. Many cannot see how foolish this work is. Many could not do anything else.

- I am angry much or most of the time.

- My drinking has increased. It helps me settle down. Or, maybe I have been a heavy drinker for some time. It may be that others have told me and I have denied it.

- I dismiss negative or critical comments from others as coming from sources lacking knowledge or insight. Nevertheless, these comments hurt a lot.

- I find others generally nonsupportive and/or lacking in understanding of me.

- I wish my marriage partner knew me better. I wish others knew me better. They just do not seem to care.

- Most people want something from me. Most relationships cost something. Most people want or expect something from me even though they do not ask. I am reluctant to pay.
- I am seldom certain that I am loved. I am not certain I am respected.
- I believe that relaxation is a waste of time and unproductive, even though I say that it is not.
- I believe that relaxation is something that I could do more.
- I am more emotional, or more sensitive, or more angry, or less happy than most people.
- I am more judgmental than most people, but I do not act on my judgments or let others know them.
- I am less judgmental than most people because being judgmental is wrong.

Second Cluster of Issues

In my family (parents, siblings or grandparents) there is at least one person who is or has been
  a. depressed
  b. mentally ill
  c. emotionally abusive
  d. sexually abusive
  e. physically abusive
  f. obese
  g. an alcohol or drug abuser
  h. a workaholic
  i. accidentally disabled
  j. divorced
  k. a smoker or an overeater
  l. chronically ill or
  m. died while I was in childhood.

Interpretation of the Issues

The items in the first cluster of issues embody some distortions of reality that may indicate damage. The more strongly you felt a response, the higher the probability of damage, as the statements in the list contain the reflections, beliefs, and thoughts of wounded people. These ideas are the kind that stubbornly refuse to go away, even when the people attempt to replace them with more rational ideas. They reflect deeply ingrained notions and beliefs that may pervade all areas of life and work.

In the second cluster of issues, positive responses indicate the probability that some damage has been inflicted. Any one of these conditions may contribute to damage. Family history, personal history, the history of relationships, and employment history provide clues to the possibility that a religious professional is at risk. There are no fixed rules for determining risk or the degree of risk. The process of discovery is an intuitive one and requires sensitivity in trying to locate the balance between individual personality and adverse circumstances. For example, the fact that a marriage has remained intact is not a certain indication that the participants are not at risk. In order to make that judgment, one would need to know a good deal more about the individual marriage partners than the longevity of the marriage—for example, information about the nature of that relationship and parts of the life histories of the two partners. Conversely, being divorced does not automatically indicate that a professional is at risk. How the person has reacted to the divorce and at what level self-awareness is present are more determinative. It is also helpful to measure the person's self-perception against the perceptions of others, and to ask whether professionals are conscious of the mixed motives involved in the choice of a religious profession. How aware of others' thoughts and emotions do they appear to be? Do they demonstrate awareness of time, place, and history? Do they seem to have a sense of the total context in which they are playing a part, or do they always put themselves in the center? Often even a brief interview with an at-risk professional will suggest a fruitful line of questioning that will produce an intuitive profile.

Wounded children feel responsible for their own wounding even when they least deserve to carry the weight of that responsibility, but when adults discover the effects and sources of their wounds they can remove from their lives a great sapper of psychological energy. For religious professionals, the need to confront and understand old wounds is usually not just an individual responsibility but a social one as well. A professional religious leader who is unaware of his or her past wounds and present defensive structures can influence a whole group or congregation and render it dysfunctional. Dysfunctional or at-risk people gather those around them who are like themselves and also help to create more people and even groups of people like themselves. Healthy professionals, on the other hand, tend to aid in the healing of those around them.

PART TWO

DROWNING IN DEFENSIVE STRUCTURES

5

NARCISSISTS: SEEKING LOVE, FEARING CLOSENESS

Narcissists live in a grandiose and exaggerated world of their own creation. They feel themselves to be unique, unprotected by parents, different from all other people, and unable to get too close to anyone. They often try to be attached to others and learn to feign care which they unknowingly substitute for genuine closeness. The narcissist is unwilling to pay the cost of true friendship, and so all relationships become merely performances.

The ranks of corporations as well as the medical, religious, and psychology professions are populated by successful narcissists. Many of them combine their defensive structure with some characteristics of the compulsive personality (see chapter 7). The drive that accompanies their woundedness often results in high achievement or an ability to produce an exciting performance. Many priests, rabbis, pastors, academics, physicians, attorneys, executives, theologians, social activists, and psychotherapists are narcissists. These persons seek to and often succeed in legitimizing their defensive structures through the kind of high achievement or exciting performance made possible by the drive derived from their woundedness. Narcissists who function at low levels often blatantly exploit others.

Narcissism is the inability to love another out of fear of death or a nonexistence akin to having no reflection in a mirror. More detailed and technical definitions will be discussed later in this chapter. The narcissist believes that safety can only exist in a situation separate from others or under personal control.

Narcissists usually judge early that their parents are not providing safety or rewarding performance. The parents have been sending confusing messages. On the one hand, the child's uniqueness is always pointed out. On the other hand, this uniqueness and talent is rewarded as reflecting on the parent, most often the mother for males and the father for females. A life-draining situation emerges. The parent is saying, "Be successful for me." Anger at the demanding parent becomes mixed with a desire to please; that is the driving force. Marriage or employment are replications of the childhood experience: Joining is seen as always extracting a cost. That cost is the self.

Narcissists are more likely to act out than to act in. The history of Derrick illustrates how narcissism affects the life of a religious professional and a congregation with whom this professional is working.

DERRICK: LOVE ONLY ME

The letter from the governing board of the Church of St. Luke to the bishop listed grievances against the new pastor and the parish secretary. Pastor and secretary had each filed a complaint about the other. Various members of the congregation added their grievances against both and, in a report, asked for immediate intervention. The board reported that things were bad and getting worse. People were voting with their feet and their pocketbooks; in other words, attendance and income were down.

The list of complaints ranged from the significant to the absurd. There was one serious charge of breaches of confidentiality, but also an accusation that the secretary was making too many errors in typing the bulletin (even with a word processor) and putting the hymn numbers on the board in the narthex without permission. The complaints alleged that Derrick, the new pastor, had not visited every member as he had promised he would do. He had changed the order of the service without the approval of the governing board and did not mow his lawn every week. In turn, Derrick complained that the property committee had not kept its promise to paint his study.

Derrick had been pastor of St. Luke for only ten months. Previously he had worked for nine years in a larger working-class parish in a medium-sized city. His judicatory supervisor suggested he might want to move following his divorce. Before this he had served a small upstate rural congregation previously served by the same tired man for thirty years. There Derrick worked for five years after his ordination. Even though Derrick was the son of successful professional parents, he loved to identify himself with and dress like "real people."

The two congregations both loved him and tolerated him, finding him a free spirit. They admired his relaxed attitude. He was privately sarcastic about the hierarchy of his denomination. A loner who liked being with people who admired him, he seldom found anyone he believed could teach him much. Nonetheless, the people of the first rural church supported anything Derrick chose to do and liked their young and enthusiastic clergyman. He became close to several younger families in the community who shared his enthusiasm. But as tasks repeated themselves, the excitement wore off and Derrick decided it was time to move on. He believed he was destined for bigger and more important things.

Derrick grew up a child of privilege. He was accustomed to being the center of attention in both his immediate and his extended family. He was musically talented and intellectually astute. His siblings and his cousins identified him as the "different" one, but the difference was generally judged to be a good thing. He was so much the paragon of his family that he was sometimes afraid to be in places where there were no other family members. Often he came to feel as if he were on display as their representative. Even as a child he came to expect this special treatment and felt twinges of jealousy if another child appeared to be the center of attention. Despite this, Derrick learned to act in appropriately humble ways when he received praise. He did not enjoy much that he was asked to do. Nevertheless, he would perform in order to receive praise. Fear and terror began to accompany his performances.

By adolescence he began to undermine and belittle his own successes. He began to search for his own performance mode that did not depend on family kudos. But he could not escape. No matter what he tried, the family supported it. But he found it difficult to be like the rest of the family.

Whenever Derrick attempted to do new things, even if they seemed easy, he feared that he would not succeed. He lived with this tension, constantly afraid of failing, refusing to work hard enough to be excellent, and always expecting adoration from others, even for less than maximum effort. The only times he was not terrified were in situations in which he perceived no competition. He became angry when authorities blocked him from doing what he wanted or when sufficient praise was not forthcoming. He often felt alone, even in his few close relationships.

He turned his insecurity into eccentricity. He resolved his internal tension by offending in the name of artistic freedom. Professionally this was manifested as an insistence on ecclesiastical-historical and liturgical correctness. He found he could keep his distance from the center by creating a center of his own. He led where he felt in control; otherwise, he stayed out of things or privately belittled those who were in control.

An ordained religious profession seemed a good choice for Derrick. Clergy had status in his family structure and in his home community. As a clergyman he could be an activist and community leader. He could have an impact on people's lives and help change the world. His family was thrilled. Going into a religious profession kept him different from his peers, who were headed toward more traditional careers that did not interest him.

At St. Luke Derrick succeeded a hard-driving perfectionist who made most church decisions himself through a little pre-meeting manipulation in order to get the vote he wanted. Under this man's twelve-year ministry, attendance and income had increased steadily. This popular pastor was a hard act to follow. Derrick decided that the best move was to assert his own style of leadership from the start.

Shortly after his arrival at St. Luke, Derrick began hearing stories about Jonathan Upberg, his predecessor. Jonathan had given the congregation his best for twelve years. He worked hard and seemed never to rest. He visited every member. If you needed him, he was there. Nearly every member had a story about being helped by Jonathan Upberg at some critical time. Even Upberg's eventual resignation from St. Luke was motivated by need, that of his wife and children who faced a crisis. Jonathan seemed the perfect pastor and human being. He loved his people and he loved his family.

In time, Derrick became more and more angry at his predecessor and began to search for some evidence that Jonathan had failed somewhere. He spent more time with those few members who expressed criticism of Jonathan. He subtly began to make comments critical of Upberg's ministry. Why didn't Upberg choose a wider variety of hymns from the rich tradition available within the denomination? Was Jonathan's scholarship really sound? Why did he refer people to professional counselors? Did he lack adequate pastoral counseling skills? Derrick felt a surge of satisfaction when parishioners began to seek him out for counseling, and he prided himself on the trust he was building. It was the approval of the few that kept Derrick going during the early months.

He began to assert himself by changing the congregation's weekly worship service. It would be done correctly and in a manner consistent with historic tradition, not in the casual way to which the congregation had become accustomed—in other words, not in the sloppy and liturgically shoddy ways of Jonathan Upberg. He selected at least one unfamiliar hymn each week to enrich the congregation, and when they asked for the old hymns he selected an occasional hymn dating from the Middle Ages. He answered criticism by saying that the changes were in the long-term best interest of the congregation and that he wanted to compensate for past neglect and to bring them up to the current denominational standards. He became critical of the small errors made by the secretary. "The worship bulletin was the most important piece of paper generated by the congregation," he told her. "It needs to make a statement about the quality, sophistication, and excellence of the whole congregation's work."

As the tension between Derrick and his staff and also some of the congregation increased, he began to express his anger. He would threaten to resign. Each time this happened, the governing board coaxed him to stay. Occasionally he would throw a temper tantrum. He often pointed out that each of his preceding parishes had been successful and that he had made a personal sacrifice to respond to the needs of the parish of St. Luke.

His anger was most visible at home, where his new wife reported that he seemed in a rage all the time. According to her, he became even angrier when she told him that his behavior was childish. He screamed, threw things, and stomped around. He would also pout, pound his fists on the arms of chairs, and bang on doors. Then he would lapse into angry silence. His behavior seemed to him both normal and appropriate.

Derrick is a narcissist. He has gotten into some professional entanglements after fourteen years in congregational work. His personality structure and defenses are manifesting themselves. He is subtly and aggressively beginning to act out. Not surprisingly, the congregation is resisting the assault but is equally irrational in its resistance. The issues here have little or nothing to do with the list of complaints.

THE MISUNDERSTOOD WORD

Perhaps no term used to describe a personality is so often used or so misunderstood as narcissism. An entire decade of American culture has been described as narcissistic. Misapplied, the term conjures up images of self-centeredness, obnoxiousness, and huge egos; it conjures up such words as egotistical, selfish, obnoxious, unfeeling, and others which suggest that narcissistic personalities are "stuck" on themselves. In fact, the narcissistic personality is almost the opposite.

Most high-functioning narcissists are anything but obnoxious. They can be quite likable and very attractive to others and can function well professionally. The narcissist is often a successful professional who is an angry trial at home. It is as if a switch were to be triggered on and off by the demands for public performance. As the former wife of a narcissistic religious professional recently told me, "Others were always telling me what a joy he must be to live with. After all," they said, "he is gracious and kind, entertaining and bright." All this was true, she reported, "except when he was at home with me or the children."

In short, contrary to popular belief, the narcissist's real problem is a deficiency in a healthy sense of self. Lacking appropriate ego boundaries, the narcissist spends most of his life keeping distance from others while feigning closeness and being unable to relate effectively to others in any satisfying manner. Narcissists are also among the most hypersensitive of human beings (Smith 1984).

The common misconception about narcissism is rooted in a misunderstanding of the myth of Narcissus. It is commonly understood that Narcissus was in love with himself. More accurately, Narcissus was unable to love anyone, including himself. All relationships became extensions of himself. The narcissistic personality is cut off from everyone else except as these others are perceived as extensions of the self. The narcissist is unable to perceive other people as real.

The Myth and Its Interpretation

Echo was a beautiful wood nymph with one failing: She was fond of talking and needed always to have the last word. Zeus found this failure to be useful. He would use Echo to keep his wife, Hera, in conversation while he dallied with other nymphs. Hera discovered the ploy and passed a sentence on Echo: She lost her power of speech except for the purpose of reply.

Shortly after Hera pronounced her sentence, Echo fell in love with Narcissus and followed him incessantly, waiting for him to speak first so she could reply. One day the youth was separated from his companions and sensed another presence. He called out, "Who's here?" Echo replied, "Here." Narcissus made several attempts to join with her, but all she returned were the same words he spoke.

She ran to him and threw her arms around his neck. He was startled and shouted at her, "Hands off! I would rather die than have you with me." Echo begged him to take her but he refused.

There were other instances of Narcissus' cruelty. Eventually a young woman prayed that some day Narcissus might feel what it was to love and receive no return of affection. Hera heard this and granted her wish.

One day Narcissus came to a clear fountain, knelt down to take a drink, and saw his own image in the water. He believed this to be a water spirit and gazed in admiration at the image. He fell in love with himself. Every attempt to touch the image met with frustration. The water's surface was disrupted. He felt shunned, became ill, and began to cry. His tears fell on the water and the image again disappeared. He pined away and died (Bulfinch 1955; Larousse 1959).

There are several variations of the Narcissus story, but the components in the version presented here are central to a classical psychoanalytic understanding of narcissism. First, Narcissus was capable of loving and might have loved Echo if the quality of the relationship with her had been unhampered or unencumbered by her curse. This suggests that his ability to return love and relate to another was impeded by Echo's inability to initiate but only to respond. Second, once the injury had been inflicted on Narcissus, he remained unable to reach beyond himself. Third, by implication, those who relate to the narcissistic personality are angered by the lack of returned love and hope that some day the loved one will feel the same as they do, loving and being frustrated in that love. Such is the narcissistic injury discussed earlier. Love is not freely given but withheld. Narcissus could not feel love from anything or anyone. The image of himself that Narcissus projected into the stream could not respond freely. He withered and died. The withholding of spontaneous love was literally a death-inducing injury.

Definition of Narcissism

Before the publication of the *Diagnostic and Statistical Manual of Mental Disorders: Third Edition* (DSM III, 1980), narcissism was a long recognized phenomenon but not an official diagnosis. With the publication of the DSM III, the narcissistic personality disorder became one of the eleven (later expanded to twelve) types of personality disorders. One researcher (Bursten 1982) indicates that all types of personality disorders share basic features of an intense narcissism (a result of early parental injury) and lack of a cohesive sense of self.

The *Thesaurus of Psychological Index Terms* (1988, 67) defines narcissism as follows: "Self love in which all sources of pleasure are unrealistically believed to emanate from oneself, resulting in a false sense of omnipresence, and in which the libido is no longer attached to the external love objects but redirected to oneself."

The current edition of the *Diagnostic and Statistical Manual of Mental Disorders: Third Edition—Revised* (DSM III-R, 1987) explains the developmentally rooted defensive structure in the following way: The personality traits of the individual continue over time to be inflexible, maladaptive, and persistent interferences with social or occupational functioning (305). In the narcissistic personality disorder, the following traits are manifested in past, present, and long-term functioning:

1. Grandiose sense of self-importance or uniqueness: for example, exaggeration of achievements and talents, focus on the special nature of one's problems.
2. Preoccupation with fantasies of unlimited success, power, brilliance, beauty, or ideal love.

3. Exhibitionism: the person requires constant attention and admiration.
4. Cool indifference or marked feelings of rage, inferiority, shame, humiliation, or emptiness in response to criticism, indifference of others, or defeat.
5. At least two of the following characteristics of disturbances in interpersonal relationships: (1) entitlement: expectation of special favors without assuming reciprocal responsibilities; for example, surprise and anger that people will not do what is wanted; (2) interpersonal exploitiveness: taking advantage of others to indulge own desires or for self-aggrandizement; disregard for the personal integrity and rights of others; (3) relationships that characteristically alternate between the extremes of over-idealization and devaluation; (4) lack of empathy: inability to recognize how others feel, for example, unable to appreciate the distress of someone who is seriously ill.

An alternative definition of the narcissistic defensive structure, and perhaps the clearest description, is that of Otto Kernberg (1975, 16–18, 227–30, 263–64). He describes narcissism in terms of eleven prominent features: excessive self-absorption; superficially smooth, appropriate, and effective social adaptation covering profound distortions in internal relations with other people; intense ambitiousness; grandiose fantasies existing side-by-side with feelings of inferiority; overdependence on external admiration and acclaim; feelings of boredom and emptiness; endless search for gratification of strivings for brilliance, wealth, power, and beauty; incapacity to love, to be concerned, or to be empathic toward others; chronic uncertainty and dissatisfaction about oneself; exploitiveness and ruthlessness toward others; chronic, intense envy, and defenses against such envy, for example, devaluation, omnipotent control, and narcissistic withdrawal.

Together these definitions capture the sense of uniqueness that narcissists ascribe to themselves and the accompanying grandiosity and all-or-nothing thinking. This uniqueness and all-or-nothing thinking are characteristic of all three major defensive structures that compose the pathology of religious professionals.

It is agreed that the roots of the narcissistic injury are largely pre-oedipal. Again, another myth intervenes. To think of the Oedipus complex as hate for father and jealous love for mother is simplistic. Like Echo and Narcissus, Oedipus's narcissistic wounds are not self-inflicted but come to him from the outside. At the birth of Oedipus, his father, Laius, is warned by an oracle that his son will kill him. Therefore, he has his son removed from the kingdom and raised by another. The separation precipitated by fearful, threatened parents inflicts this narcissistic wound (Bettelheim 1982).

AT THE BEGINNING

A narcissist's attraction to a religious profession usually has less to do with a sense of call than with a belief that some excitement can be found within the system. Narcissistic clergy are often those who want to attack the system from the inside. They are attracted to the drama and action of the religious system.

Narcissists are human beings who have been so conditionally loved that they believe themselves to be totally unloved. They counter this by an exaggerated drive to be loved. Even intense loving from another person only fills their inner emptiness for short periods of time. The private life of the narcissist is often one of intense and extreme emotion, which fluctuates between the extremes of passionate sensuality and intense anger, neither of which satisfy. These people are in love with love and driven to action. Narcissists experience chronic emptiness and a feeling of being unloved.

Bright narcissistic persons tend to embrace professions that are high in autonomy and visibility or on political or creative frontiers. Jobs like these offer public exposure, reduce the need to confront authority, and are safe from threatening interference. Narcissists perceive as threat just about anything that gets in their way. Narcissistic physicians and psychologists, for example, resent the interference of third-party reviewers and are angry at government's or insurance firms' attempts to make them accountable. Narcissists love minority institutions, causes of various sorts, glamorous, dramatic, or dangerous jobs, jobs perceived as powerful, and the limelight in general. There are as many narcissists among the ranks of powerful majorities as there are among the ranks of the Ku Klux Klan.

Narcissists want to be kings or queens. They perceive being at the top as being out of harm's way. They want their own monarchies and are often content to begin with small ones. The purpose of the organization matters less than the position the narcissist can hold within it. They crave total unquestioned authority. For that reason, and because they are easily bored, narcissists seldom last long in jobs. They can be fine during the honeymoon period, but day-to-day detail is not for them.

Another characteristic of narcissists is to equate action with accomplishment. Their greatest fear is death or a nonexistence, akin to not being seen. By remaining in motion at the center of their own universe they imagine they can stave off death. Activity other than their own is disregarded as meaningless.

Histrionic and Antisocial Components

Two additional defensive structures almost always appear to a greater or lesser degree as part of the narcissist's total makeup. The first is a histrionic component and the second an antisocial one. This latter was formerly referred to as sociopathic or psychopathic. Each of these is actually a separate defensive structure that can be but seldom is manifested by itself without the narcissistic component; in religious professionals it is always seen as part of narcissism.

Those with histrionic defenses constantly need reassurance, seek approval or praise, and are uncomfortable when the spotlight is not on them. They present themselves in a highly dramatic way, demonstrating much emotion and grandiosity but feeling it only shallowly.

The second defense is more insidious and causes more harm to others. Antisocial people do not avoid others, as the name may imply. Rather, they act with no internalized sense of right and wrong to shape their consideration for the needs of others. Just as the compulsive is a person with an overly strong conscience that inhibits action, so the sociopath is a person with an underdeveloped conscience. Antisocial personalities simply satisfy their own needs and desires without regard to others. It is no longer surprising to find sociopaths among professional ranks. We have all seen media coverage of criminal behavior by religious professionals. It is consistent with the pathology, however, that the more antisocial a person is, the greater is the likelihood that he or she will be caught despite attempts to avoid publicity. The antisocial person seems to have an aversion to being honest; this type is compelled to dishonesty, abuse, or deception of others.

In their low-functioning form, these persons are among the ranks of the chronically criminal. But we also find low-functioning narcissists with a small admixture of antisocial defense structures. These people can become abusing clergy, therapists, physicians, and psychologists who chronically lie to their peers, their marriage partners, their friends, and those in authority. They are impulsive, planning only for the next thing that they want. They frequently abuse substances in the same ways they abuse people. They make bad credit risks for associates as well as for banks. Many higher-functioning antisocial persons gravitate toward jobs in which lying and distortion are a way of life, such as certain kinds of sales work.

The combination of the antisocial with a low-functioning narcissist is probably not treatable, just as narcissism alone cannot be treated when the level of functioning is too low. Since narcissists characteristically believe that there is nothing wrong with them and that problem sources are always external, narcissists do not seek treatment and will not respond to it.

Narcissists Among the Clergy

Narcissistic clergy operate on the force of personality, and they tolerate no real peers. They may court superiors in order to see themselves as peers of superiors, but they are not interested in genuine exchange. Narcissists are fickle in friendship, judge others in terms of usefulness, and reject people with bitter criticism, a criticism they always spare themselves. *Idealization and devaluation* is the technical term for their process of boom-and-bust courtship of others.

Religious systems are perceived as places of excitement, action, growth, and exhilaration by some narcissists who also feel that there they will be left alone with a captive audience and given power to compensate for their damaged self-esteem. Over time they may resent committees, conventions, and workshops because they move too slowly, fail to give them enough attention, and remind them that they are part of a whole.

In spite of the fact that religious leadership has often seemed conservative and stuffy rather than flamboyant, there have always been narcissists among the ranks of religious professionals. Their proportion has changed from time to time depending upon the general culture, including such factors as its tolerance for eccentricity and acting out and its permissiveness. When Madonna becomes more of a cultural model for the society than Mother Teresa, we have begun to make the climate of culture one more conducive to narcissism.

People have been given permission over the last fifty years to be more flamboyant and even to act out in socially acceptable ways. Less socially acceptable forms of acting out by large proportions of the population are quite recent additions to our culture.

The role of the clergy before the aftermath of World War II was relatively constricted. In the mainline church, divorce among clergy was frowned upon through the 1950s and clergy drunkenness or anger in public almost unheard of. In the more adventurous period that followed, not only did acting out occur more often, but experimentation within religious systems grew, making the ecclesiastical profession, including the mainline churches, more attractive to narcissists.

Even before the revolution of the 1960s, however, narcissism was present within the mainline church among those clergy who manifested private cruelty and abuse while maintaining the public façade of correctness and compulsivity. Ingmar Bergman's *Fanny and Alexander* illustrates this type of hypocrisy.

When acting out happens with consistency over time and creates only a small crisis here and there, it can precipitate tremendous growth and maturing for high-functioning narcissists. Among the ranks of the most successful and mature religious professionals are former dysfunctional narcissists who have paid attention to the mess they were making of their lives and the lives of others.

MONICA: A NARCISSIST'S LATER YEARS

We have looked at a narcissist at the beginning of a career as the board examined him and as his career unfolded. Now let us examine another narcissist at career's end.

Monica Johnson is a sixty-one-year-old religious professional serving on the staff of a large congregation in a suburban setting. Her congregation is considering terminating her employment because she performs poorly and cannot get along with the laity. They think she pays too little attention to their ideas because she always does things her own way. The congregational board listens to all sides and agrees with the complaining membership.

Monica, however, has all the right excuses. Her brother who is very close to her is dying. She is also (she thinks) more expert in her field than the laity and believes that her attempts to lead were thwarted by a small number of disenchanted members. She knows she can appeal to the caring hearts of the board members, for they will consider it an act of cruelty to fire a sixty-one-year-old professional who probably will not be able to find employment elsewhere. Monica's employment history has been unstable throughout her adult lifetime, but now her age will assure her of employment throughout the remainder of her career.

Monica is well entrenched in her narcissism, and the circumstances of her life have not broken her defensive structure in ways that permit her to mature beyond them. Her denial is high. This suggests that she is not aware of her anger and hostility.

Monica's perception of herself is grandiose and exaggerated. She sees herself as both more capable and better educated than she really is. This is not uncommon among people who are somewhat narcissistic. They have difficulties with their own identity. Monica considers herself the authority and therefore has difficulties with all other authority figures. As is common in her generation, Monica does not reveal emotion but maintains absolute privacy regarding personal, professional, or family problems. As her withholding becomes increasingly unusual in a more open society it takes more of her emotional energy to maintain privacy and fend off perceived attacks. The remainder of her career will be spent fending off people she sees as hostile in a world she does not understand.

Monica does not have all the skills she needs in her job. When she goes to workshops to learn, she always thinks that she knows more than the presenters. This makes learning impossible.

As Monica was growing up, her parents' inflated sense of importance affected their children. Monica also thinks she is better educated than other religious professionals, although the reverse is true. She has no graduate degrees beyond her seminary degree.

Monica is a lonely person who tends to isolate herself. When the board decides to retain her, they will recommend that a committee supervise her during the remaining years of her employment. This will require extra work of the laity involved. An act of kindness like this to a dysfunctional professional postpones some other congregational work and appears to be rewarding and maintaining an illness. Monica was unknowingly holding the congregation hostage until she got her way. The congregation's decision is not unusual in religious systems: What else can be done with an older dysfunctional professional who is unwilling to accept criticism, get help, or otherwise cooperate in making an unworkable situation workable?

A study of narcissistic clergy completed in 1985 and replicated in 1989 found low-functioning narcissists in professional positions in large parishes. They all believed they were functioning adequately despite evidence to the contrary. Whenever a board or a committee believed them not to be functioning, they always had a string of excuses. Ask a narcissist why something is going wrong and he or she is always able to tell you why it is someone else's responsibility.

Why do low-functioning narcissistic professionals often finish their careers in large congregations? Perhaps the membership of a large congregation is qualitatively different from that of a smaller congregation and is more tolerant of professional eccentricity. Or perhaps large congregations want only ritual function from their clergy and seek less activity for themselves, putting the spotlight on the leader. Another characteristic of narcissists in the religious professions is that they are very fond of name dropping, defining their importance by the number of important people they presume to know. They are quick to tell you that these "famous" people always agree with them.

One discouraged bishop admitted that older narcissists in large congregations were an embarrassment to his denomination but would simply need to be tolerated until they retired. What he failed to recognize is that narcissistic clergy are reluctant to retire and probably would seek to remain in some sort of active position as long as they are able.

When we find a disproportionate group of the narcissists in the religious professions to be older people, we need to look at the particular issues faced by narcissists as they mature. These share much in common with the developmental tasks isolated by such theorists as Kernberg.

CHANGES NECESSARY FOR MATURITY

Otto Kernberg (1980, 121–53), borrowing from the work of others for some of his insights, has listed the tasks required of a narcissist as he or she moves from the first half of adult life to the second. These tasks are required for the narcissistic components of all developmentally damaged people:

1. *The resolution of excessive envy and rivalry.* Until this issue is successfully resolved, the narcissist is not able to enjoy vicariously the pleasures of others. When this issue is resolved, "they become able to watch without envy their children growing up" (Klein 1963, 16–17).

2. *The recognition of eventual death.* This is manifested as increasing consciousness of the terminal nature of life. One accepts limitations and gains a kind of "constructive recognition that imparts security to life and work" (Jacques 1970, 45).

3. *Narcissistic investment.* Around the middle of adult life a narcissist either wakes up or begins moving gradually toward increasing rigidity, compulsiveness, or intolerance, in a kind of pathological institutionalization which results from almost any long-standing, unchanging situation. Dysfunctional marriages become similarly institutionalized: They continue because they have continued. In the case of narcissists, they become increasingly committed to their own narcissism. On the other hand, if narcissists focus attention outward toward others, they can better appreciate, admire, and affirm themselves (Eissler 1975, 589–646).

4. *A shift in time perspective.* The person approaching middle age begins to look to the past more clearly as well as to the future. There is a modification in the way the life cycle is perceived. It is quite normal to have a renewed preoccupation with one's childhood and adolescence,

but during this transition the perspective is clearer than in the transition from adolescence to young adulthood (Kernberg 1980).

5. *A consciousness of external and internal change.*   There is a sense earlier in life that "I change and everything else stays the same." In the mid-life transition, the sense is altered to "I change and so does everything else." Consciousness of the changes in one's children, marriage, job, hometown, and so forth have begun to be perceived differently (Kernberg 1980).

6. *A consciousness of the limits of creativity.*   In middle age there is increasing awareness that other people's achievements will in all probability surpass one's own. This is not to be interpreted as entirely negative or counterproductive, although it can have unfortunate results; rather, it signals a beginning in one's ability to relate to and accept others in a more loving manner than was possible earlier in life (Kernberg 1980).

7. *Acceptance of limitations to internal change.*   The altered time consciousness also carries with it the increasing knowledge that one's character has a limited ability to change. Increasing stability can result from the acceptance of these limits. "To accept the inherent conflicts in love and marriage and to contain them in a stable object relation is perhaps the major task of middle life" (Kernberg 1980).

8. *Coming to terms with aggression.*   The narcissistic male is particularly called to address the issue of aggression. He perceives his environment as exaggeratedly hostile from the beginning. Middle age is the time to accept the fact that life is not fair (Kernberg 1980).

9. *Loss, mourning, and death.*   This issue concerns how one copes with losses or the need to begin again. Middle age is a time when loss or a sense of serious failure at work, social life, marriage, or relationships with close friends or children can either be dealt with effectively or be life shattering (Kernberg 1980).

10. *Oedipal conflicts.*   The process of becoming an individual is related to the psychoanalytic concept of the oedipal conflict as well as with various parent-child issues. Middle age is a time to rethink these issues. Representing them differently and distancing oneself more from parents can either result in greater freedom and less commonality or in less freedom and more commonality (Kernberg 1980).

6

DEPRESSED/DEPENDENTS: AFRAID TO BE ALONE

Imagine feeling powerless over the events and relationships in your own life. Imagine having to accept this powerlessness as the way things are. Imagine always looking to other people to make life better and, with all hope of real change being denied, looking only for readjustments and compromises. This is the life of the Lake Wobegon people who are taught not to take themselves too seriously and not to want or expect too much out of life. Hope is inhibited, boundaries are tight, and things will not get much better. This is a life of "don't expect too much."

Depressed/dependent persons have no confidence in their own emotional strength or intellectual abilities. They feel powerless over events and relationships and are often willing to sacrifice anything, including their wants, needs, or themselves, for a sense of belonging equated with safety, security, and love.

They participate in and perceive their marriages, families, or careers as if they are interacting with the families they did not have as children. Relationships and systems become overlaid with fantasy until they cannot bear the burden of the need. Then, inevitably, come hurt and disappointment.

While persons with this defensive posture are more likely to act in, they may often engage in actions that appear to be acting out, such as sexual promiscuity. A depressed/dependent sometimes becomes promiscuous to pay for closeness or duration in relationships. An angry depressed/dependent is like a child screaming for attention.

DAN: I FEEL SAFE HERE

Dan was thirteen when his disabled and emotionally abusive mother died. Following her death, he went to live with his sister, who had both children and problems of her own. He found no warmth or welcome there. Dan's father, who was physically abusive and an alcoholic, had died when Dan was eight years old. He still has a vivid memory of his father forcing him into scalding bath water while he screamed to be let go. He is haunted by his mother's regular threat to put him into an institution if he did not behave.

Following his mother's death, Dan was befriended by a local clergy-person. He was encouraged to participate in church youth activities and spent considerable time with the pastor, feeling a part of both his family and the church. He recalls the proud day when he was given a key to the church so he could help the sexton, coming and going as he pleased. He spent many hours alone in the church. He would go there directly after school, let himself in, and lock the door after him. He says that during his early adolescent years he felt safe and secure only when locked alone in the church. Not surprisingly, Dan decided to become a pastor. Because of his youth activities and his apparent enthusiasm, he became the darling little boy of the judicatory officials. He loved it and felt safe.

In his first congregation he was already operating at a high anxiety level. There was so much to do and he did it all. It was an older con-gregation with many parishioners in the hospital or homebound. He made daily hospital calls and visited forty-six shut-in members every month. He initiated or attempted to initiate any program the board suggested, but only those suggested. He wanted to do what was asked. Within a short period of time he was tired all the time. His wife complained and encouraged him to get out of the ministry. This made her the enemy. He screamed and stormed at her. Dan never wanted to fail the safe and loving church family that had taken him in.

Within eighteen months he was failing to maintain his impossible schedule and had become physically drained and depressed. His bishop, believing the parish to be too demanding, quickly secured another position for Dan with a younger and more enthusiastic congregation. Instead of enjoying the more active parish, Dan worked even harder and was ex-periencing increasing periods of depression. He perceived his wife to be even more hostile and avoided her.

He got depressed and teary so often that those close to him became angry and refused to provide the sympathy and caring he thought he needed and deserved. To him, depression seemed normal and others were supposed to give him sympathy. To others he seemed like an overly demanding child, unable to cope with adult life. A battle shaped up between those who loved and supported Dan and those who counseled him to seek help. His sympathizers, whom he considered the "good" people, helped him keep the tension-filled status quo firmly in place.

An actively involved laywoman was among those who befriended Dan. She spent increasing numbers of hours volunteering at the church and expressing support for him. Their relationship grew closer and they became physically attracted to each other. Following their mutual declaration of love and intention to leave their respective marriages, Dan went to his bishop. The bishop told him that he could remain ordained if he stopped the new relationship. After one week he said he could not do it. Dan was asked to resign from the professional ministry. If he failed to do so, he would be removed. He was both surprised and hurt.

Dan had virtually no identity other than as the adopted child of the church. He had never become a separate human being; there was almost no "self." The church's authorities judged his behavior and failed to see that it stemmed from developmental damage. Dan was sent into what for him was "outer darkness," in which he was too fearful to venture much beyond his home or his narrowly defined job tasks.

There are those in the church who could not function in the larger world without significant external protection. Like Dan, they have put all their eggs in an ecclesiastical basket, trusting that they will be cared for if they work hard and responsibly. These persons are the products of severely dysfunctional families and have known little other than dysfunction. It is an act of cruelty to put them out even when short-term supportive services are given to them. But many religious systems have no alternative.

THE EMERGING THIRD STRUCTURE

Several years ago I believed that only two defensive structures could be identified among religious professionals. I looked upon the depressed/dependent structure primarily as underpinning for the compulsive structure. This seems no longer exclusively true. I now see the depressed/dependent structure as separate. I also see it increasing. Depressed/dependent persons with narcissistic and compulsive secondary features are pursuing church professions in greater numbers.

This is not a new defensive structure. Depressed/dependent persons have always been a part of the general population of at-risk individuals. That there should be more of them in the professions is probably attributable to changes in the culture and in role expectations in the religious system. It may also result from the ways in which candidates for religious professions are screened. The more a system sets guidelines for entry, the greater the likelihood that compliance becomes normative among candidates. Present candidate selection processes may encourage and support dependency by screening out would-be rebels and iconoclasts.

Since careers have been in large measure a matter of free choice rather than inherited, chosen by birth order, designated by gender, or determined by economic necessity, frequent matches occur between career choice and personality structure. This is not surprising; it parallels what we have known in a system of romantic love for partner choice: It often means choosing a matching pathology. One might argue that since there is about a 50-percent failure rate for marriage by pathological choice, the failure rate in career choice ought to be about the same.

It seems that this may be both true and not true. Perhaps as many as two-thirds of those who choose a profession such as psychology, medicine, or teaching may say that they would not choose their profession if they had to do it over again, although this has not been documented so much as deduced. While I have never seen a study of clergy, it is not unusual to talk to clergy who have been in the profession for over fifteen years who say they would not make the same choice now. Studs Terkel (1974) reports dissatisfaction with work at all levels in this culture on a massive scale, so we can certainly not generalize that only those professionals at risk become dissatisfied. The key to career dissatisfaction over time probably lies in the mismatch of personality structure and career. But we should not underestimate the role played by unrealistic expectations and exaggerated ideals.

If depressed/dependents were not present in high numbers among religious professionals until recently, where were these people? In religious systems, they formed the army of volunteers. They willingly did the work of the committees, the educational programs, the many tasks that the religious professional and the boards deemed important. Depressed/dependent personalities followed the leaders, believing their contribution important simply in the doing. They thrived on the intimate attention from the leaders, who, at the time, included many narcissists and compulsives. Depressed/dependent persons do not see themselves on the cutting edge but rather as part of the larger and safer system that provides a place to belong, a sense of the family. There now appears a tendency for the volunteers to become the professionals.

The Depressed/Dependent Personality

The depressed/dependent is not driven in the same ways that narcissists and the compulsives are driven. They cooperate rather than direct. Their values are largely traditional and received and change slowly. Some tend to be more depressed than dependent, while others are the reverse. Often they are seen as healthy people because they are not threatening, and we expect religious professionals to be noncompetitive and cooperative like these people are. What is missing for professional function is a healthy drive that leads to creativity, new ideas, vision, and a program. The defensive structure, when leaders are predominantly of the depressed/ dependent group, creates a passivity that can be stultifying within a system. A supervisor once taught me that it is always easier in therapy to slow someone down than to speed someone up. The depressed/dependent needs speeding up.

Depressed/dependents grow up expecting that high performance, to other people's specifications, will generate its own reward. Reward comes in the form of fairness, nurture, and, most especially, safety. The cost for safety and love is self-sacrifice. Among depressed/dependents either the self is weak and poorly defined, or a self never emerges as a separate entity but is enmeshed with the group ego of the original family. In the first instance, the self gradually disappears without substitute, especially in the context of a relationship with a narcissistic or compulsive personality. The individual merges with whatever he or she is attached to. The price is not deemed too high when safety and security are at stake. In the latter instance, there is no separate self, but a part-self which easily attaches to an other and remains enmeshed in the new system. If the depressed/dependent is the product of abuse, the self will attach only to another abusive relationship or a series of them. This is a paradox of human development and relationships. While depressed/dependent persons want a safe and nurturing relationship, they cannot ever get one until the defensive structure gives way to maturity. Even if fortune attaches these persons to healthier adults, they will seek to undermine them until the original condition is replicated.

Some depressed/dependent people describe themselves as coming from supportive families who cared for and nurtured them. They may continue to relate too closely to their parents or siblings. They are willing to sacrifice the self for the sake of this family and cannot imagine a life apart from them. Even in marriage, the new partner is often taken into the larger family as a sort of adopted child. This belonging is equated with safety, security, and love. The depressed/dependent cannot imagine that these qualities exist beyond the family.

Women Among Depressed/Dependent Professionals

The ordaining or setting apart of women in religious professions has inadvertently contributed to the increasing numbers of depressed/dependent professionals. Greater numbers of women adopt and accept nurturing roles and characteristics. Greater numbers of women than men respond to abuse with a kind of learned helplessness or depression. More men, it seems, respond by becoming rigid or aggressive. Even though the majority of religious professionals continue to be male, greater numbers of women are active in the work of the congregation.

In religious systems with a history of women as professionals, there seem to be three identifiable generations. When a religious system first opens the professional doors, it finds pioneers who have been standing on the other side aggressively seeking to come through. These new and pioneering professionals are consistently revealed to be more intelligent and more emotionally mature than their male counterparts in the profession. Shortly afterward a second generation emerges. These women are not unlike their counterparts in intelligence, emotional maturity, or self-image. Then follows a third generation. Clinical interviews and psychological testing reveal the third wave of women to be more traditional in their understanding of role and function. Often these women have been working in the church for many years and the decision to pursue a church profession was an evolutionary one. Most are married with children in varying stages of development. They have often been surprised to realize, as a result of contact with women clergy, that the profession is now open to women. If they have careers, they are careers that have been home to depressed/dependent personalities in the past: social work, elementary education, or nursing. As the numbers of these women increase in proportion to the total ranks of religious professionals, they will contribute to the changing character of the whole.

Jean is a candidate for ordination in a major mainline Protestant denomination. She is presently in her early thirties, married, and has two children. She graduated from a small liberal arts college with a social work major. She has a history of successful employment in social services both as social worker and as administrator. She has a long history of volunteer service to her church. Over the past two years, her church work has evolved into a part-time position.

Jean is poised, bright, socially skillful, articulate, and extroverted, but with an insecure core. She attempts to cover this insecurity with poise and her considerable social skill.

Jean enjoys her role as mother and says that she is learning more all the time. She particularly knows that she has to concentrate on herself and her own growth as much as on the behavior of her children. The more she understands about herself, the fewer problems may occur with the children. Jean seem to be living the stereotypical American dream of career combined with perfect parenting. But there is some anxiety under the surface.

Jean's parents were divorced about three years ago after a three-year separation and approximately twenty-five years of marriage. Since the separation, her mother has successfully participated in an alcohol rehabilitation program and is recovering. Her father is remarried and is a workaholic. The candidate says that her mother's alcoholism was hard on her but that it took an even greater toll on her sister. We can trace the roots of Jean's anxiety to her developmental years as a child in an alcoholic home.

Jean makes the most of her ability to combine intelligence with personality and is energized by working with people. She thinks concretely. She feels the need to give socially correct answers so as to be seen in a favorable light. This concern may lead her to some defensiveness in those situations where she is being scrutinized or challenged. She is reluctant to talk seriously about her personal problems.

Jean knows that she needs to be clearer about where she is going from here. She wants to be ordained but is not quite clear about how this desire fits in with the other priorities of her life. It is difficult for her to balance family needs and personal needs. She feels pulled at different times by the needs of her church, the needs of her family, and her own needs. She sees a problem in balancing priorities. Jean has trouble finding time for herself.

Jean is an example of a religious professional who appears to have her life in order. In reality, she does not. As her children grow and exert more pressure on her, as professional demands increase, and as there are inevitable stresses in marriage and family, the denial defense, which presently can be maintained in a reactive and dependent structure, may collapse and leave her depressed. Her traditional life structure is being maintained at a cost to herself.

Products of Severe Dysfunction

There is another group of persons with a depressed/dependent defensive structure who are the products of more severely dysfunctional families. These sexually, emotionally, and physically abused adults are seeking to enter religious professions in greater numbers. The structures of their original families were punitive, abusive, or depressed, and the parents never bonded with their children. The children formed no self-image or only a weak one. This makes for great difficulty in maturing. Depressed/dependent people of this group view their own marriages, families, or careers as the sources of the safety, love, and nurture they never had. Inevitably they are frustrated because the realities cannot satisfy their exaggerated needs.

Catherine has been married for fourteen years and is the mother of three children. She enjoys her role as mother but describes her marriage as in need of constant attention. She says that her husband is mostly passive and inattentive, ambivalent about her career choice, and prone to occasional bouts of anger. She says that he only hit her once but she never knows when it might happen again.

A number of years ago, she and her husband participated briefly in counseling sessions. Her husband stopped going to the sessions because he believed the pastoral counselor was siding with Catherine. She continued in the counseling relationship for about one and a half years.

About a year after the sessions began, her counselor told her that he was becoming attracted to her and was not certain he could any longer be helpful. She was feeling the same about him although, despite the intense emotional attachment, there was no actual physical involvement. Such relationships are common for religious professionals. Both the pastoral counselor and Catherine needed separate therapy, but neither sought additional help after the counseling stopped. Her counselor told her he was sorry about what had happened. Neither Catherine nor her husband have ever mentioned counseling again.

Catherine's father was an absent workaholic and her mother was a dependent and depressed woman with damaged self-esteem. She says that she is much like her father; like him, she received both undergraduate and graduate degrees with a near perfect academic record.

Her marriage is and will be problematic and abusive until she is able to address her family issues and her unresolved feelings about her former counselor, whom she still idealizes. Right now she says that she wants to help people and to be part of a loving system. She tends to take on more than she can handle and says that she needs to slow down and reflect more. She describes guilt as her motivator, finding roots of guilt in her parents' marriage, with a bossy and verbally abusive father and a depressed and dependent mother. Catherine's dependency will probably keep her from seeing her own issues and will inhibit her growth for some time. This candidate is a cautious caterpillar trying to keep her own process of transformation under tight control for fear of the consequences. There is a tension between the desire for change and the fear of its repercussions.

Another religious professional has the following story: Peter was married for about eight years and is the father of three children. The history of his marriage was abusive. His former wife was an abused child and witnessed physical violence between her own parents, so she also became abusive. She would attack Peter in the presence of the children. Peter was active in a conservative Protestant denomination and was dismissed as a candidate following his divorce. He has since been ordained by a mainline denomination.

This professional experienced considerable psychological trauma around the time of his separation and divorce. He still carries the unresolved emotional pain from the abusive and demeaning relationship with his ex-wife.

THE DEPRESSED/DEPENDENT
DEFENSE STRUCTURE

More women than men exhibit a depressed/dependent defense structure. We cannot be certain, therefore, whether depression is depression or some combination of repression and oppression that results in depression. The depressed/dependent person most often manifests a pattern of dependent and submissive behavior that involves several of the components listed in the DSM III-R (1987). A dependent person may be unable to make everyday decisions without an excessive amount of advice and input, often allows others to make most important decisions, may agree with people even when he or she knows they are wrong for fear of being rejected or disliked, initiates projects with great difficulty, volunteers to do things that are unpleasant or demeaning in order to get other people to like him or her, feels uncomfortable and sometimes helpless when alone, may go to great lengths to avoid being alone, is devastated or helpless when close relationships end, hesitates to end even manipulative or abusive relationships, is frequently preoccupied with fears of being abandoned, and is easily hurt by criticism or disapproval. This latter hypersensitivity is common to all defensive structures.

The depressed person often feels helpless, has little appetite, and has trouble sleeping. Often he or she will fall asleep easily but wake during the night and feel tired and unrested in the morning. This person suffers from chronic fatigue, little or no creativity, impaired decision making, and poor concentration. At these times self-esteem is particularly low, irritability high, and motivation stifled. A depressed person simply is not interested in much of anything.

The primary goal is to remain safe, to belong, and to be loved. For this, the depressed/dependent will perform without question, always being loyal, persevering, and dependable. It is little wonder that such people are valued as volunteers. What they fail to see is the cost to themselves for their loyalty to others.

Depressed/dependent professionals want more from others than others can deliver and are often taken advantage of. They keep hoping that other people and the world in general will be different than they are. Their denial is strong and is matched by hope for change in others. Depressed/

dependent professionals believe that their loyalty and faithfulness will maintain their safety. Such people invite abuse and victimization. They are often tolerant beyond human boundary and capacity, acting out of duty alone.

When these persons are functioning at a low level they are quite difficult to work with. As they do not want to displease, they often do little and take very few risks. Their style is a highly reactive one which waits for clues to a safe next step from those in authority. A low-functioning depressed/dependent personality probably should not be ordained. We can minister to them in our parishes, but we do not need to make them leaders in order to elevate their self-esteem and demonstrate our level of caring.

7

COMPULSIVES:
SCARED STIFF

Imagine a life consisting only of battles to be fought and struggles to be grimly endured. Imagine a life with the never-ending, overwhelming responsibility to impose order on chaos. In such a life where acceptance must be gained by pleasing people, one must remain ever vigilant and on guard. Rules of life are somehow to be decoded and, once decoded, followed. These rules change frustratingly and one must adapt to the changes. It is as if understanding were to be found in a Life Owner's Manual, if only one could find the current edition before they change it. Imagine a life where ambivalence cannot be tolerated, and the drive for clarity is seen as the goal. Imagine a life in which one believes that only by attending to the very small will one solve the large. Imagine a life where there is no "whole picture" but only disconnected pieces, so that one must complete the puzzle without having all the jigsaw bits. Imagine a life of ceaseless tasks. This is the life of the compulsive personality.

Compulsives have thought processes that work like computers, collecting, filing, sorting, storing. They are always processing data and cannot turn off the mental machine during their waking hours. They believe that to act or react in any given situation means simply pulling up the file and replicating the suggested behavior data. Like the character Data on *Star Trek: The Next Generation*, or his predecessor, Mr. Spock, they perform well but are confused when new rules, emotions, or the illogical are introduced to them. Also like Data, they have a quality about them that is not quite real. Wilhelm Reich (1949, 199) called them "living machines." They are stiff and lack spontaneity, fluidity, and flexibility. When they have a thought or a worry, they cannot get it out of their minds. They believe they win acceptance only by constant correct performance, and so they live in fear of making a mistake or an error. A physical, emotional, and cognitive rigidity characterizes this defensive structure. These are professionals who are "scared stiff."

This defensive posture is equally likely to act out or act in.

GAIL: COUNT ON HER EVERY TIME

Gail is a forty-one-year-old senior staff clergyperson of a seven-hundred-member congregation. Her predecessor retired three years ago and the congregation insisted that she stay on in his place, although the move forced a male fellow member of the staff to resign. It was clear to Gail that he had wanted the position. She thought that the two of them had worked well together as junior staff.

Gail had a reputation for being very bright and extremely efficient. She never missed a detail or a promised deadline. She enjoyed the full support of her former supervisor, who enjoyed his own role as her mentor. Some other staff said that they did not feel they could get close to her and found her somewhat rigid, but this was seen as a small price to pay for such a capable professional. Some of them said that all bright people seemed aloof to them.

After she took the new position, things began to happen to Gail. She became increasingly rigid and socially more aloof. Congregational leaders attributed this to the stress of the job change. Judicatory executives, hoping to show faith in her, asked her to serve on more committees. There she participated efficiently and effectively, always being prepared on every detail of each document to be discussed. She was elected to a national board and appointed its chairperson. Her loyalty to the parish never slackened. She visited the hospital faithfully, even when told it was unnecessary when a parishioner was undergoing a minor procedure. The membership knew that she cared very deeply for them all. Her pace was unrelenting.

Gail never discussed herself or her problems with staff members. Occasionally she would call on her former mentor and discuss some of the pressures she was feeling. He told her that she was working too hard and needed to begin thinking of herself and her own needs. She took comfort from the advice but never followed it.

During this period, Gail would wake between three and four o'clock several mornings a week with thoughts about the tasks of the coming day racing through her head. In the third year she woke more and more often, going over in her head the problems she expected from each coming encounter. She would think of all the things she might forget to do and then review the errors she believed she had made the preceding day. She made plans to correct mistakes with a telephone call or a note. She particularly worried about the work of the national committee, because she thought this to be her chance to make a significant contribution to the whole religious system. Other committee work worried her too; in fact, although she never mentioned it, she worried about almost everything in her career. Gail was tired and did not feel well.

Gail was doing a nearly perfect job and it was making her sick. When staff members asked about her overwork and fatigue, she said she was fine and just needed a short vacation. When she returned from one of her short breaks, the intensity of her pace returned within a few days.

Gail is the younger of two children and a native of a small mid-Atlantic industrial city. Her older brother left home after high school and has lived a kind of catch-as-catch-can life, moving from job to job and never settling down. He has had bouts of alcohol abuse and was married three times before the age of forty. His children from these various relationships remain with their respective mothers. Gail's father is seventy-nine years old and in poor health after a lifelong career as a factory worker. Her mother is seventy-five years old and has never worked outside the home. Neither parent finished high school. Gail remembers them as quiet and steady, attributes that to her indicate strength.

Gail excelled in school both academically and in extracurricular activities. She edited the high school paper, sang in the chorus, and played in the band. In her family congregation she began teaching young children when she was fourteen years old. She sang in the adult choir and accompanied the children's choir. At age sixteen she took a part-time job to help with home expenses. Adults looked to her for help and admired her accomplishments.

She graduated cum laude from a highly regarded small liberal arts college and became a junior high school history teacher, a position she held for ten years. As a faculty advisor, she worked with the chorus. At her congregation she headed the education committee. Although not entirely happy with her job, she gained the respect of faculty and administration alike. All the while she lived with her parents and took responsibility for them as they aged. At the end of her tenth year of teaching, she abruptly resigned and applied for admission to a seminary of her denomination and to candidacy for ordination. Her credentials were virtually impeccable.

As a candidate she said that the separation between her commitment to her congregation and her career had always bothered her. By becoming ordained, she could bring these two worlds together, expand her knowledge, and make a real contribution where it counted. She excelled at seminary.

Gail seems to be a model professional adult. She lives by a traditional set of rules and by a code of conduct more common to earlier times. Although never openly judgmental, she is privately angry at the laxity of others around her. She tries to be positive about everything. She supports her parents, her brother, and a young niece and nephew. She works hard, always putting in more hours than anyone else on the staff of her congregation. Her loyalty to family, friends, and congregation are unquestionable. She is very serious and seems unable to relax. Indeed, her attempts at recreation and relaxation typically result in more hard work. She cannot *play* tennis or volleyball; she *works* at tennis and volleyball. Gail is, in fact, a model of adulthood without being adult at all. She is only imitating a version of adulthood that she came to believe in during her grim childhood and adolescent years.

Gail is single but she has had several relationships, all with men who needed her emotional support more than they could offer support to her. Now she claims to be in love with another religious professional. He is twenty-four years her senior, separated, and the father of three grown children. She is certain that they will eventually marry. Until then her traditional rule book is being ignored, and this causes her inner tension.

CONTROL: NEVER LOSE IT

Rigidity is the word most often used to describe the compulsive. They even physically look stiff and are constricted emotionally. Compulsives live in the middle range of emotion, believing that any expression of extreme emotion is "crazy" or out of control. Even their cognitive processes are rigid and limited, lacking playfulness or flexibility. The compulsive even has to work hard at spontaneity. Compulsive humor is in the early adolescent stage. A compulsive talking to a child sounds like the imitation of an adult. In fact, a compulsive is generally an adult imitating an adult.

Control is another word often used in connection with compulsives. They not only work very hard to be in control of themselves, but they believe that it is important to control everyone and everything else. A compulsive believes that there is one way to do things—their way. They seldom delegate for fear that the task will not be done properly. One religious professional I know regularly made a round trip of three hours to purchase eucharistic wafers and altar candles because he believed there was no one else he could trust with the task.

When compulsives are not working, they feel they are not being responsible and therefore have no worth as a human being. When compulsives feel that the volatile core is touched, they think they are going crazy, even though there may be no real threat of severe mental illness. What they fear most is loss of control evidenced by release of emotions. The compulsive needs such a high degree of control because they fear chaos as greatly as the narcissist fears nonbeing.

An old saying about compulsives is that they work harder doing things right than at doing the right things. This means that procedure is more important to them than results. Compulsives worry about almost everything. They have only a single priority level—high, which indicates their inability to separate the essential from the inessential.

Some compulsives are driven by outside demands and are unable to prioritize these demands. They frenetically execute other people's wishes in what seems to be nearly random and jerky sequence. They are like voice-activated mobiles set into motion by uncoordinated voices, or like television sets with a chimpanzee at the remote controls. When the switch is turned on, the voice trips the action and the compulsive cannot escape but does as bidden until, but only until, another button is pressed.

Everything is a high priority, as they cannot separate the essential from the inessential. It is as if their minds were radios with circumstance choosing the stations. Each station is tuned by the forces outside the compulsive. When a station is tuned, the compulsive cannot escape. As all other circumstances interfere with the reception, they have a difficult time concentrating on the station because of background interference from all other stations equally unchosen by the compulsive.

The compulsive is a person with an anxious and constant internal drive, though an undifferentiated one. Compulsives believe that there is something very important that they need to do. They often report that in their late teens or early twenties they went to a youth group retreat or to church one Sunday, and it suddenly occurred to them that the Spirit had called them to be missionaries, or religious professionals, or directors of education for a congregation. Divine calling comes in very handy for the compulsive, who feels that his or her work can be nearly anything but it must be supremely important. What has happened here is that the internal anxious drive has been reflected back as if God were a mirror. The compulsive does not understand how self-deceiving undifferentiated drives can be.

A sample compulsive response to a Rorschach test may be, "These are two geese flying somewhere." Compulsives are persons who are flying somewhere but do not know where. Then God, or a cross, or a revered religious professional appears and they conclude that God has somehow clarified the direction.

Compulsives learn early that anger, rage, and sexuality are bad. They even deny the existence of such drives within themselves. But the volatile core of their drives remains and causes anxiety that the drives will get them into trouble. They have grown up in emotionally starved homes and believe that they are not to become angry or depressed. All the emotions felt when the compulsive was younger have been put away, because the compulsive's early observation of the adult world has led him or her to believe that only crazy people show emotions. To set aside emotion also means to conceal or deny joy, exhilaration, or ecstasy. What emerges is a human being with a limited emotional range masking a volatile core, which is forced below the surface. Sometimes it is closer than the compulsive would like to believe or acknowledge.

Interview with a Compulsive

Interviewing compulsives can be an exercise in frustration, when the emotional core is tapped and immediately (compulsively) concealed. Here is a sample interview segment:

INTERVIEWER: What things make you angry? Does anything make you angry?

RELIGIOUS PROFESSIONAL: Oh, that's right. I understand. I'm with a psychologist. You're supposed to ask me things like about anger. Let me think. Yes, what makes me angry is the *New York Times*.

INTERVIEWER: What makes you angry about the *New York Times*?

RELIGIOUS PROFESSIONAL: All the trees that are used to make the paper.

INTERVIEWER: Why does that make you angry?

RELIGIOUS PROFESSIONAL: Because God put all those trees there to be revelled in and appreciated as a part of his creation. They are being destroyed and uprooted. Tearing those trees out of the ground makes me angry.

These are not comments about the environment at all, but strong sexually loaded connotations of phallic trees turned into newspaper. There is something being manifested that the compulsive does not want to be visible. Attempts to interpret the input would be useless. The professional is not angry at the lumber or paper industry, or publishers, or the destroyers of the environment. He is just angry. This anger is mollified by the sense that God is involved and has called him to spiritual work.

The Ministry and the Compulsive

How is compulsiveness manifested in the professional ministry? Until recently, studies of clergy have suggested that the compulsive is the single defensive structure to be found in religious professionals. A summary of the research suggests that at-risk religious professionals show opposition and are emotionally distant, personally conflicted, and engage in activity to compensate for strong feelings of personal inadequacy (May 1967). My own work, on the other hand, has identified at least two types of defensive structures and a combination of the two, accounting for a third. I suspect that earlier research was actively attempting to identify a single strand. Many researchers were unfamiliar with defensive structures and their personality manifestations. As has already been said, all defenses arising from emotional damage have common threads.

The times and the culture have changed the leadership profile of the religious system over the years. The activist 1960s and early 1970s, with their insistence on freedom and spontaneity, forced the compulsives' fear of untidy hair and uncontrolled protest underground. The civil rights movement, Vietnam and the antiwar movement, and later feminism and ecological concerns gave a church platform to narcissists, who in former days would probably not have considered a religious profession, and who, had they done so, would have been denied a place within a preserve of compulsives. Now, once more the shift is toward more compulsivity and less narcissism.

BERNARD: HOW COMPULSIVES
ARE MADE

The stiffness and rigidity of the compulsive results from learning very early that acceptance is contingent upon correct performance. The compulsive believes that angry judgment will follow the incorrect execution of assigned tasks. There is at least one parent in the house of the future compulsive who is perceived as insufficiently strong to generate a feeling of security and safety.

Bernard, who is in treatment, is an example of such child raising. Bernard's father was a rigid and judgmental man who expected his children to perform better than all others. The fact that he had not done so himself seemed irrelevant to him. Bernard remembers his father working with an adding machine at the dining room table night after night for fear that he would not get his own work done and would lose his position. Bernard's mother was depressed. He can barely remember her and thinks of her as invisible, unable to protect him from his father.

Bernard has very few fond memories of childhood play with friends. Instead, he recalls scoldings from his father. During adolescence, Bernard "fit in" by associating himself with those students who were popular.

They convinced him that he, too, was popular. Even though he was unsuccessful in student elections and was not nominated for the fraternity of his choice, he remained driven.

By his early adult years, Bernard had advanced in his profession under the tutelage of a man who was very much like his father. Bernard feared the man and felt tension before every meeting with him, but he believed that only by pleasing him would he find success. As he approached his middle years, he reported chronic bouts with insomnia, persistent tension, and several episodes of a mild depression each year. He studied these symptoms and carefully monitored his own schedule and diet to avoid them. He even developed a computer program for this purpose.

Then Bernard collapsed into a major depression. He could not make himself get out of bed or go to work. His treatment sessions increased and he began an antidepressant medication. His compulsive defensive structure had collapsed and he could no longer keep all the "shoulds" in his life going, even with a computer to help him. Clearly he needed to make life decisions and alter his way of life. Eight months after the major depression began, Bernard decided that he wanted to remain in the professional ministry but in a totally different way. The religious profession was no longer to be the center of his world. Instead, it became something he could do well and make a living at, but something that would leave him time to spend with his children. He now works in a smaller congregation and is much less frightened.

Bernard is like most compulsives. Judgment follows the slightest perceived failure. Compulsives work hard at everything. Working hard becomes more important than the task worked at. It is important for them to work harder than anyone else. Even relaxation and achieving sexual pleasure are tasks to be done correctly. Any failure will result in rejection or nonacceptance. Therefore compulsives appear to be always wary, unemotional, uptight, and chronically anxious. Although they are seldom happy people, compulsives' attention to detail and meticulousness nevertheless has value.

Anxiety is a word often used but seldom defined. To describe it as chronic tension is to describe the symptom and not the condition. The condition itself is rooted in fear. Anxiety always involves an attempt to escape. It is psychologically running away from something fearful in the past that one is projecting onto present circumstances. Anxiety is the condition of chronic fear that the future will work out as the past did. The anxious compulsive comes to believe that he or she can run to avoid a reenactment of past scenes or can keep all things balanced, and he or she will be safe.

Compulsive religious professionals have to believe that someday, some-how, the religious system chosen will become what it ought to and should be. They exert much control to ensure that the system follow their dogmatic rules. They even carry balance and fairness to extremes, for it is difficult for them to see that most things are really unfair and out of balance.

When the compulsive professional's defensive structure explodes, re-pressed and denied feelings are exposed, thereby revealing a person who believed him- or herself to be in a safe, just, and balanced system, and who has been betrayed. The individual has been rendered incapable of working and feels driven by fear of dismissal or reprimand. When the lid blows off it confirms to the compulsive that emotional outburst and acting out really are a form of "going crazy." Religious professionals are particularly hard hit when they crash, because they have had to believe that in the church they have found the one safe and important place on the planet. They do not know where to turn next. For a long time this is very painful. They must come to grips with the fact that they are part of the human race and most of the human race pumps gas, works at banks, or works for companies. Sometimes the door to maturing only opens when anger at the religious system yields to collapsed defenses and then to depression. Compulsive personality crash is popularly called burnout. Somewhat paradoxically, depression is the entry point to health and wholeness.

Another way for a compulsive occasionally to reach wholeness is through an unconditional love affair in which they are accepted for being and not for doing. This is not a recommendation that compulsives should have affairs but an observation of the importance of unconditional love in allowing certain compulsives to mature. Usually such love comes early with teenage romance.

A compulsive is somewhat tragic. The tragedy is that a person should have spent a whole life trying to understand the shoulds, the should nots, and the oughts. Such people always play by the rules and always become frustrated. Therefore, when an acting-out episode occurs, it is usually a big one in which long pent-up emotions explode. We have all heard stories of the kindly school teacher who robbed a bank one day and left town in a stolen car never to be seen again, or the accountant who stole $350,000 and left town with the wife of his largest account, or the religious professional who suddenly cracked up and chased parishioners down the street while brandishing a baseball bat. We are shocked and entertained by the incongruous collapse of the superresponsible and secretly delighted in their downfall, if only because we sense that our own control rests more lightly but works better. But in cases where the explosion comes, a depression cannot be far behind.

ROBERT: A COMPULSIVE IN THE MAKING

Robert is an example of a young compulsive candidate for a religious profession whose inflexibility and rigidity make him a potentially at-risk professional. Robert is a college junior whose life has been framed by one traumatic event. His father died when he was twelve years old, approximately six months after his diagnosis of cancer. This event changed the history of the family and the candidate forever. The results are most visible in the young man's self-described critical nature and in his obvious immaturity.

Robert is the older of two children. His mother has not married again. Even when his father was alive, the family did not communicate well with one another, and since the death the remaining members have been largely isolated and private.

Robert has dated only sporadically and reports few long-term friendships. He had just moved to a new school before his father's death and knew few people there. His mother is a native of the Midwest and ever since her marriage appears to have had difficulties adjusting to her New England environment. An overly close attachment exists between mother and son, which has been exaggerated by both the death of his father and the acting-out adolescence of his brother. Robert describes his mother as overprotective. He has become someone his mother can count on. He looks to her for authority.

His involvement in the church and desire to be a pastor are also tied to his father's death. This does not invalidate his choice, but it means he may have difficulties when the church inevitably disappoints him. Rigidity or black/white thinking is symptomatic for Robert. He feels that the religious system has accepted him when other people did not.

Robert is suspicious and has significant difficulty trusting others. In speaking with him, what comes through most strongly are issues of identity and self-esteem. Rigidity, chronic anxiety, and denial have followed his lack of self-esteem and crippled his academic performance and career choice. While he is not quite completely stuck, he is close.

Robert understands some of these issues. He says that he needs to work at how he deals with people. Some people have told him that he is a nice guy, but he does not really believe them. He says he is always afraid of getting hurt, and so he has to go to obsessional extremes to figure people out. Other students have told him that he can find five to seven things wrong with everyone.

CRITERIA FOR DEFINING A COMPULSIVE

A compulsive exhibits a pervasive pattern of perfectionism and inflexibility in various ways; he or she may fail to finish tasks because personal standards not met. compulsives show a preoccupation with details, rules, lists, order, organization, or schedules to the extent that the major point of the activity is lost. They also insist unreasonably that others submit to exactly their way of doing things, and are unreasonably reluctant to allow others to do things because of the conviction that they will not do them correctly. Compulsives are excessively devoted to work and productivity to the exclusion of leisure activities and friendships.

A compulsive shows several forms of indecisiveness: decision making is either avoided, postponed, or protracted (for example, the person cannot finish assignments on time because he or she spends too much time ruminating about priorities). Compulsives are overconscientious, overscrupulous, and inflexible about matters of morality, ethics, or values: They restrict expression of affection, lack generosity in giving time, money, or gifts when no personal gain is likely to result, and are unable to discard worn-out or worthless objects even when they have no sentimental value.

Compulsives suffer excessively from guilt feelings because they have been made to assume too much responsibility in their own development. They are chronically anxious and manifest a general nervousness which may make them appear to be the most attentive of human beings. These persons cannot cope with the sheer size of things, so they reduce everything in size to its smallest pieces. They believe that by managing all the pieces, the whole will eventually be achieved. They often hear every word and miss the point.

Compulsives are not free people. "In fact, they feel exceedingly uncomfortable in circumstances that do offer them a whiff of freedom" (Shapiro 1965, 40). Compulsives do not enjoy vacations; they plan them and work very intently on them, but they never find them fun. It is little wonder that when a compulsive relaxes the defensive structure collapses into depression. They appear burned out. It was not the stress of the job that did it to them, however; it was their own personality structure. They cannot relax even when given the opportunity.

At low-functioning levels or when the defensive structure is beginning to collapse, compulsives may exhibit some paranoid features. Sometimes awful material that compulsives know about themselves is projected as if it is coming from others, thus putting the compulsives at the center of the world with a spotlight shining on them. Everyone seems to be judging, everyone can see what is happening, and it is all bad. At this juncture compulsives may attempt to solicit the help of friends in keeping themselves secret from others whom they believe to be dangerous. Among those seen as dangerous may be the entire congregation, or religious authorities, or other peers. If the professional has been somewhat high functioning in the past, these paranoid features may be a clue that an intervention is possible and necessary in the near future.

The majority of religious professionals and of the professional population as a whole are some combination of compulsive and narcissist. These persons, when mature and functional, are prized by religious systems as successful and their contributions to the system welcomed. At lower levels of function, they can be quite difficult for congregations and hierarchy alike. The strong and unconsciously driven desire for autonomy, with its roots in fears of closeness and further hurt, requires years of professional attention before maturing mollifies it.

Both the narcissist and the compulsive are stuck. One has poor impulse control and grandiosity, while the other is fearful and unable to act spontaneously. Often professionals combine these two defensive structures in virtually equal amounts. In fact, this combination comprises probably the largest single group of professionals, including religious ones. High-functioning professionals who combine narcissistic and compulsive traits have a great potential for addressing their issues in a healthy way, but they may encounter many difficulties in the process.

DAVID: TIMELY TREATMENT

David is a religious professional in his early thirties who serves as a specialist in youth work. He was accepted for his current post on condition that he pursue a program of personal therapy because of a messy divorce and public conflicts with staff persons in his prior congregation. He is an example of a common combination of the compulsive and the narcissist. The narcissistic drive led to frequent sexual and aggressive acting out and to problems with a senior staff member. Problems began because there was room for only one king in his former kingdom. His grandiosity led him to want to be adored and praised for his greatness. He still says that he will settle for nothing less than being the best. His compulsive self contributed to his academic and musical accomplishment; it also caused him to be a perfectionist and a cleaning fanatic. He never rested, and he incessantly drove those he claimed to love. His professional style combined seduction and directiveness. He was convinced there was only one correct way to do things and believed that everyone else worked too slowly.

Early in his treatment, he married a woman with three children. This relationship began while both were still married to their former partners. She was an active volunteer in a neighboring congregation, and they met in the course of religious activities involving several congregations. The new marriage, unresolved issues from two former marriages and from a failed professional partnership, fears related to his ethical and moral breach in becoming involved with his new partner, issues related to the start of a new marriage and new job simultaneously, and the adjustment to stepchildren—all these factors slowed his therapeutic progress.

David is the older of two children of a dysfunctional family. He fantasizes his parents as weak and ineffectual. His strong feelings against his mother run deep and are rooted in early childhood. He describes his house as always dirty and disorganized. Early in his life manifestations of his obsessive-compulsive nature emerged. He says that the only place in the house that was organized was his own room. He cleaned his room daily, a practice which he continues in his present home. He is always straightening and dusting in his spare time. He becomes angry when there is clutter or dirt.

David did not even like his theology to be messy. He embraced a fundamental religiosity during his adolescent years. Early unsuccessful relationships and impulse-driven sexual activity added to his fears that he was out of control. He struggled all the more for order and predictability in his life. Like other compulsives, he was externalizing controls that he was unable to manage himself.

David's family has a history of depressive symptoms, including accomplishment inconsistent with ability, a general lowered energy, and low motivation. David runs, sometimes compulsively and sometimes impulsively, from a fear of being like his depressed family. He has already experienced a breakdown of his defenses and sank into a depressed period during which his professional functioning was limited.

David's compulsive defense conceals a depressed core. He does not know his own baseline and has driven himself since childhood to perform at a high level. He seems always to be observing himself functioning and judging himself to be succeeding or failing. He uses an intellectualizing defense and could not connect his internal life to his cognitions. Since he had to have an explanation for everything he viewed, he saw emotional health as the product of correct behavior. Sexual and aggressive acting out in the form of affairs and temper tantrums, and physical acting out such as breaking chairs, were a part of his life. This was largely hidden from the congregation but was well known to those close to him. As a high-functioning narcissist he regularly became enraged at perceived insults from wife, professional associates, and, more recently, stepchildren. His pseudoempathy carried him for some years, but there was no real empathy.

David is now changing and the manifestations of his narcissism and compulsivity are lessening. David is achieving insights into his depressed core. He is beginning to establish boundaries between himself and intimates or parishioners. He is less impulsive and less likely to act out. His reality orientation is improving. He is working on establishing internal controls and relying less on the external rule-boundedness of a fundamental faith system.

Three to five years is a typical length of treatment for personality restructuring of at-risk personality-disordered professionals. It will be important that David complete this process now, rather than wait until he hits his next projected crisis. Such a crisis will come as he approaches the middle of his adult life. The pattern is typical for the narcissistic personality. David has a good chance to attack the issues and emerge as a capable professional now when he is needed because of the decline in the quality of church professionals.

This relatively young professional will contribute significantly to any profession he chooses when he has successfully completed therapy. The very factors that put him at risk also hold the possibility of exciting and mature functioning in the future, because the compulsive or the narcissist-compulsive combination conceals the strength of a capable professional behind the damage that keeps him or her from functioning.

8

BORDERLINES:
RAGE AND SEDUCTION

A few high-functioning borderline persons have recently entered the ranks of religious professionals and a few more are on the way. Either the screening committees of religious groups and the faculties of theological schools do not know how to recognize borderlines, or they knowingly admit them out of desperation, kindness, or hope that they will change. This chapter is also motivated by hope for change. Religious institutions simply should not be taking this kind of risk. We will all pay a price if it continues. While borderlines share some symptoms with the other three defensive structures, they manifest them at an entirely different level of intensity.

A borderline personality is a significantly dysfunctional person, both in relationships and in career. If borderlines appear to be functioning, it is because they have found low-stress jobs where they are protected from threat. This protection must be thorough, for the threshold of perceived threat is quite low. Circumstances may have permitted them to complete courses of study or hold low-stress jobs for brief periods, but they do not belong in a religious profession. There are a few people who habitually fluctuate between borderline and low-functioning narcissists or depressed/dependent. They may pass for simple narcissists or depressed/ dependents, but they are not.

We can expect to see more borderlines wanting to enter religious occupations (Mehl 1992). Certainly some candidates are clearly so dysfunctional that committees do not hesitate to reject them, but the high-functioning borderline has become a problem. When institutions sorely need professional personnel, they grow soft in their judgment. They hate to say no. A stern judgment may harm a candidate and even ruin a life. Committees fail to realize how much more havoc is created by introducing borderlines into the already troubled system.

There is another reason for the profession to beware of borderlines. Low-functioning narcissistic clergy, when found guilty of parishioner abuse, have most frequently chosen their victims among women and a very few men who are at best low-functioning depressed/dependent personalities with strong manifestations of the borderline personality.

A case of abuse often involves a borderliner and a borderlined. When they come together they are both moved to a lower level of functioning. In some ways both the abuser and the abused are two sides of the same borderline coin. At best, the abusing professional is a low-functioning narcissist with borderline features. At best, the victim is often a low-functioning depressed/dependent with borderline features. These two meet as one seeks help from another too sick to offer help.

It is the role and function of the certifying system to ensure the health of its professionals. Unfortunately, however, it is often only after the damage has been done that the system discovers a problem. Adequate assessment and a willingness to say no will help over time. Until then, we must clean up the messes as best we are able and provide the support we can.

Joan was only nine months old when her mother died of cancer. The fear of abandonment is a human being's greatest fear, far worse than the fear of rejection. Death is the ultimate abandonment, and for a young child the death of a mother is a wrenching trauma. Joan has no memory at all of her mother, and yet the abandonment theme has been with her all her life.

Joan's father turned over her care to his sister who lived some distance from their home, and after that he rarely saw her. Joan's aunt already had two small sons aged three and five, and no bond with her replaced the one Joan had formed with her mother only to have it tragically terminated. Joan's development came to a tragic stop.

Joan followed a pattern of successive short-term attachments into her early thirties. "I've had over thirty sexual partners," she said flatly at our first session. If any feeling came through in the early stage of Joan's therapy, it was anger. She was angry at her mother for leaving and angry at herself because she believed that in some way she caused it to happen. She was depressed and hostile. Each new relationship seemed hopeful but ended painfully in a endless reenactment of her first tragic separation. The pattern continued through the early stages of psychotherapy.

ABANDONED ON THE BORDER
OF ACCEPTANCE

To understand the fear of abandonment is to understand borderline defensive structures. Sometimes the abandonment has been superficially less traumatic than Joan's. It can be anything from abandonment by mothers who choose to have their children adopted to temporary abandonment of sick children to hospitals. In all cases, trauma has interrupted adequate bonding with the mother so that the borderline remains detached and alone. The borderline defensive structure has its roots in very early, very primitive, and very basic human needs that were not met. This fear of abandonment, coupled with the certainty that it will happen, precipitates the borderline's heady combination of rage and need. The borderline seems to say "I love you/I hate you" simultaneously.

From the first encounter with a borderline, one is struck by the anger and seductive need lurking beneath their consciousness. Many borderlines have been physically damaged or sexually abused. The church attracts and holds a hope for the emotional connection that these persons have yet to make. They may become the victims of more abuse, this time by clergy, or, having embraced a religious profession, they may themselves be the abusers. They are both victim and victimizer. In part this is because the primitive defenses of the borderline lead to a regular breakdown of the fragile boundaries that exist between themselves and others. Because we tend to respond to those who respond to us, the borderline condition is deceptive, making us believe that the person functions better than the severity of their condition would suggest.

Otto Kernberg sees similarities between borderline and narcissistic patients but notes that they have different pathology. Narcissists present themselves as individuals who do not appear to have difficulties with their own severely disturbed behavior, while borderlines appear to have such difficulty (Kernberg 1980; Watkins 1977). Both structures result from similar processes, namely, inadequate and unhealthy relationships to mother. For both borderline and narcissistic conditions the ability to connect with others is damaged.

Narcissists have a developed id, ego, and superego structure. They have ego defenses. They are generally able to work, often have an adequate sense of reality, and can function successfully. Although their relationships tend to be tumultuous, they can maintain long-term relationships with certain other personality types such as depressed/dependent persons (Kernberg 1975). Like borderlines, narcissists sometimes abuse, have fluctuating highs and lows, and demean other people. The borderline defensive structure differs from that of the narcissist in that it has no psychic mechanisms for self-protection and makes major use of denial. A borderline's relationships are always tumultuous and often sado-masochistic. Borderlines react as if they are allergic to relationships (Gordon 1984).

Where is the border that gives borderlines their name? It is that thin line between psychosis and neurosis. Psychosis is defined as the total absence of boundary and object relations, while neurosis consists of maladaptive patterns in an otherwise normally developed personality. A borderline, therefore, sometimes operates in reality as we perceive it and sometimes totally out of it. Sometimes borderlines know where their and other people's personality limits are located and sometimes they do not. The chief characteristic of the borderline defensive structure is that, having never completed the separation-individuation process, they keep repeating that developmental stage in miniversions over and over. That is why they form such inadequate connections with other people (Watkins 1977).

The narcissist is a damaged but relatively developed personality who also repeats the separation-individuation process over and over to no avail. Like borderlines, narcissists cannot relate to other persons. They fear both losing their own autonomy and joining others. The narcissist is stuck between lacking adequate relationships and fearing them, but his or her emotional coupling and uncoupling is on a more mature level than that of the borderline.

RUTH: AN INTENSE LONELINESS

Ruth is an example of a high-functioning borderline personality who is able to work successfully for short periods of time with the support of long-term individual therapy. She would not be able to do this work without therapeutic and systemic support.

Ruth is a religious professional in her middle thirties who is functioning with moderate success in a part-time position in a low-demand small working-class parish. Some financial support from a small inheritance enables her to maintain independence. As the result of an automobile accident and subsequent surgery, she sustained some neurological damage to her knees and elbows. She is chronically overweight and reports extensive allergic reactions to foods and medications. She has been in treatment for five years.

Ruth is the older of two children of a dysfunctional marriage. Her parents were divorced when she was two years old. She lived with her grandmother for about a year and a half and then returned with her younger sister to her mother's new home. There is a family history of depression, suicide, alcoholism, and at least one reported diagnosis of schizophrenia. At least two relatives have been hospitalized for depression.

There is strong evidence that Ruth was sexually abused as a child, but she can only remember fragments of the episodes, ones that occurred before she was five and that thus further inhibited the formation of a stable self. Sexual abuse continued through Ruth's middle childhood and seems to have stopped when she reached adolescence. Perpetrators of the abuse were both her father and mother as well as her paternal grandparents.

Ruth is socially underdeveloped and has had no significant long-term relationships. She fantasizes about a relationship and exaggerates the intensity of friendships with males with whom she is only newly familiar. She has regularly mistaken social support for potential romantic involvement. There is yet no evidence that she can engage in and maintain a successful relationship or friendship. Her reality orientation, while improved, continues to be impaired. This hinders her professional functioning and her interaction with peers. In sessions she will report meeting new people and finding them interesting, but within a short period of time, she stops mentioning them. When asked why, she reports some specific disappointment in them. She is angrily judgmental of almost all her peers, yet feels they neglect her.

Throughout her young adult life the terror of abandonment has been played out both in fantasy and in reality for this patient. Two years after Ruth arrived on the scene, the professional she was working with resigned. His leaving devastated her.

Ruth's parish is supportive and appreciative. Most of the membership are over sixty years of age, and she may see them as parent substitutes, which may ultimately help her to mature. Recently she has been able to function adequately for increasingly longer periods. In the past she fluctuated constantly between depression and intense anger. Now she remains easily threatened and exhibits a damaged self-esteem. Sometimes her reality orientation and ego function are also impaired.

It is very difficult for a therapist to work with a borderline like Ruth. She is so bent on reenacting the disappointment and abandonment of her childhood that she does her best to keep from trusting her helper. The level of trust becomes so fragile that everything the therapist says is reinterpreted as a judgment on her. She wants to be told she is hopeless so she can say that one more person has abandoned her. A therapist may find it impossible, because of the nature of borderline pathology, either to accept physician referrals of borderlines or to refer them. Fear of abandonment can never be left out of the picture. Obviously, borderlines require long-term therapy so that they can build up trust very slowly with many small victories and losses along the way. Ruth, for example, seems now to be fragmenting or becoming dysfunctional less frequently, but her therapy is far from complete. Ten years of therapy would not be unusual in such a case.

As the case examples suggest, a borderline exhibits an unstable mood and cannot maintain a stable interpersonal relationship. Relationships follow a pattern beginning wonderfully and inevitably ending terribly. This is the idealization/devaluation structure similar to the one we find in the narcissist, only more severe. Chronic weight problems and sexual promiscuity are the chief forms of impulsiveness and acting out in this defensive structure.

Borderlines manifest intense anger and appear out of control for no apparent reason. They become angry when least expected. Those who choose to support borderlines are in for a rough ride, because they never know from one encounter to the next whether they will find the borderline depressed, anxious, or ready with a scorching attack. One thing is certain: Should any attempt be made to get too close to the borderline, the relationship will probably terminate in a short time.

Borderlines are chronically empty and lonely. In their intense efforts to avoid abandonment, they may talk of suicide and be uncertain of who they are, where they are going, or what they believe. They also seek to drive others away in order to confirm that they are justified in fearing abandonment. Sadly, borderlines will not be able to function in the long term in a religious or any other profession; and religious professions, for all their generally desirable compassion, would do well to be on their guard against them.

PART THREE

Treading as Fast as Possible

SYSTEMS AND
RELIGIOUS PROFESSIONALS

Religious professionals are involved with at least one system, whether it be a congregation, a regional or national office, an academic faculty, or the staff of a counseling center. In most religious groups a second system, marriage and family, is also a part of the religious professional's life. This chapter discusses the unconscious dynamics of both systems and their action and interaction on the religious professional.

Imagine an ideal world in which there is no repression, no denial, and no unconsciously driven dysfunction in religious professionals or the congregations to whom they relate. It would be a world in which children are children and adults are adults. There would still be difficult problems and traumatic life circumstances. Accidents would still happen, but they would be fewer in number. There would still be misunderstandings and times of confusion. There would even be disagreements and impassioned arguments, but these would be firmly grounded in reality. Focus on the present would be so well established that there would be few difficulties in knowing what to do, what to be, or how to respond. There would be clear visions and goals and, along with them, clear understanding of how to reach them.

But this is not an ideal world, and the reality of the present is cluttered with the wreckage of the past with all its unresolved issues. To complicate matters, there is a systemic or group unconscious, which is often more powerful than individual consciousness and inhibits clear vision. In this chapter the dynamics of the systemwide unconscious in religious systems will be discussed.

At any point in the life of a religious system, there is balance or imbalance between the dynamics of working and not working. These exist side by side and operate simultaneously within the religious structure. Work and nonwork dynamics in religious structures differ slightly from those operating in a counseling setting.

Many church professionals serve in parishes in which candor is in short supply, while gossip and hasty judgment abound. Church administrators engage in problem solving only when driven to it, and so intervention is postponed until those needing it no longer have the energy to care about the outcome. Administrators seem to hope that problems will simply go away or that they can be avoided. The church system is not designed to deal with emotional dysfunction. From candidate selection through retirement, emotional health is supposed to be delivered by magic. All this colludes in ways that set the stage for the church professional eventually to falter.

The psychodynamics of the congregation profoundly influence the actions of the professional. There is always the danger of falling into an unconscious step in a dance that is more distorted and magical than real. If we understand group functioning from a psychoanalytic point of view, we are better prepared to understand how groups formed around religious principles function. In religious groups, for example, *tribal* notions often interfere with the formation of open communities and help to maintain closed ones.

This chapter is constructed on several principles. First, a group or system is not the same as the sum of the individuals who make it up. Second, groups or systems, like individuals, have both conscious and unconscious lives. Third, a group's belief system is different from the varied belief systems of the individuals who comprise it. Fourth, individuals are affected to varying degrees by membership in a group or system and become different from what they are apart and alone.

THE EFFECTS OF TRIBAL GROUPS

In the 1921 classic *Group Psychology and the Analysis of the Ego* ([1921] 1959), Freud laid the groundwork for much thinking about systems that was to follow. Eventually this type of thinking flourished with such theoreticians as Kurt Lewin and Wilfred Bion. Lewin's work in turn eventually emerged as family systems thinking with the work of Salvador Minuchin (1974), Murray Bowen (1978), and Jay Haley (1971). These latter tended to move away from the psychodynamic orientation of the earlier theoreticians. In this chapter we return to the original psychodynamic base via the work of Bion.

Individuals cannot grow and flourish apart from groups to which they belong and with whom they can identify. The family, which is the first group in a child's experience, is the prototypical group. Ideally it is here that a child learns about relating. In the family the child develops the ability to postpone pleasure, and from the family the child also learns something about love and aggression and is exposed to civilizing techniques. This early experience with the family becomes the foundation for the child in relating to other groups and moving from egocentric concerns to other directed possibilities.

More recent theoreticians have pointed out that it is common for boundaries between family members and between generations to be unclear. It is quite common for individual identity to be almost lost within the family. Enmeshment is a common term for this process. In an enmeshed family one does not know where one person begins and another ends. It is as if there were a single ego for the entire group. One can easily imagine how an undifferentiated individual from an enmeshed family exports damaged development to all later group relationships.

The drive to belong is universal. C. S. Lewis describes it as the drive to be part of the inner ring (1980, 54–73, 93–105). The postmodern time with its lack of center leads to an increasingly common sense of alienation. Since we are all looking for our own tribe, we attribute tribe-like qualities to all the systems with which we associate. The pattern may be seen in membership rites, rituals, practice of exclusiveness, the choosing of designated leaders with special privileges, the confirming of birthright membership, and use of adoption-like rituals for new members, which offer the promise of equal love and a secret language. The drive is so strong that often those who are outside will form their own tribe and create a new inner ring. This inside made up of outsiders takes on the same characteristics as the rejecting tribe.

Religious systems are tribal in their structure. They are structured around what analytic theory calls the central illusion (Freud [1921] 1959, 25–31). The central illusion of the tribe is that the head loves all members equally while the members know each other to be unequal. In Christian or Jewish congregations Jesus or Yahweh is the head and loves all members equally. Since neither Jesus nor Yahweh is very tangible, the central illusion is often distorted. In some congregations the religious leader is perceived as having a special association with the head, which places the leader in an unequal and superior position relative to the other members. When the leader replaces part of the function of the head by becoming the source of equal love, the leader becomes a sheep dressed in God's clothing.

It is then almost axiomatic that a cycle of throning and dethroning of leaders will go on in a tribe. The leader is perceived as superior, attacked by the members, removed from leadership if not membership, and then because a godhead alone without human embodiment seems unrealistic and unsatisfactory, a new leader is chosen. The system for gaining and disposing of leaders is magical and symbolic, often distorting reality to confuse the actual with the ideal and the symbol with the symbolized.

THE NATURE OF A SYSTEM

All systems are structured to stay the same. They are not built for change. Even congregational systems that are deliberately experimental and unique have developed a stable tribal identity around their uniqueness. Belonging begins with self-identification as different. This is often achieved through having been excluded and discovering why. Without difference and exclusion there would be no belonging. The need to define and abolish differences may be the primary issue to be addressed by individuals and systems for the next generation. "Who are we?" is the second question we ask, but it always follows the first question: "Who are we not?"

Early in life, we learn what price must be paid to belong. We also learn how much energy it takes to balance the drive to join with its paradoxical opposite, the resistance to joining. Brownies, the Boy Scouts, a church, a club, a marriage, or a social movement—they all lay claims to us. We are dragged into a lifelong tension between the drive to belong and the drive to be separate. Whatever balance we strike from the tension will manifest itself in our working style, our gender roles, our values, and our family dynamics.

Religious systems, unlike some other tribal systems, strive to be both inclusive and equal in the treatment of members. Within many religious systems, inclusivity often takes the form of support for minority and women's rights. But what does inclusivity mean? Does being inclusive weaken the system by making it too diverse and too varied to hold together the way exclusive organizations do? Does cohesiveness lie in exclusion alone? And if so, how can an exclusive system ever be a just one? If the ideal goal is only limited inclusiveness, how can the godhead be perceived to love all humans equally? The religious community as it defines itself may itself be an illusory ideal.

In order for countries such as the United States, Sweden, South Africa, Iran, or England to exist there need to be persons who are defined as outside the citizenry of these countries just as others are inside it. These former are excluded. Freedom for South Africa means, more precisely, freedom for South Africans. The right of membership in a nation does not imply that all that nation's citizens are equal, but it does imply that they will or should be treated as if they are equal.

Differences between mutually exclusive groups are as much a matter of faith as of definition. It has been well established by Freud ([1921]

1959), Goffman (1963), Hoffer (1951), and others that exclusivity is a necessary component for system survival. This is not to say that all exclusive systems are strong or indeed that they survive. Rather, exclusiveness is a precondition to, not a guarantor of, strength and survival. Witness the eating clubs of Princeton or the secret fraternal societies that flourished during the first half of the century. As long as a society tolerated the exclusiveness of sex as a membership criterion, these groups were strong and very much alive. Today they are less important and less powerful.

In a culture that regards the membership criteria of race, gender, sexual preference, lifestyle, and creed as violations of human rights, those organizations that have opened their doors to all are struggling, while the closed organizations that continue to practice a simplistic exclusiveness remain stable and proceed as if little has changed. They are dinosaurs in a new world. But they are noticed. They are clear about who is in and who is out, while the rest of us flounder in our attempts to act exclusively in order to define membership while at the same time not excluding any gender, race, or creed in the process.

All systems (institutions, corporations, churches, families, organizations), therefore, are built on a foundation of exclusiveness. When someone is "in" someone has to be "out." Exclusiveness attracts us and gives us definition, helping to form our judgments. Attempts to be more inclusive always threaten the whole of the structure.

What is the place of the prophetic voice? Prophetic voices always and of necessity come from outside the system or, once in the system, seek to redefine it. But systems delude themselves into thinking they are prophetic when they are not. For example, a system's devotion to human rights controls its own change by making certain that the radical voice once excluded is now present, but it also contains that voice at the lower levels of the system. When that radical voice becomes too powerful, it is purged and reestablished at an even safer lower level. The voice becomes a token one, purely symbolic as an expression of concern, but rendered powerless within the system. The expression of concern becomes sufficient apart from any action. This introduces rank within a system and thus is antithetical to the leader-loves-all-equally model that characterizes religious systems.

In conclusion, what is necessary for the strength and maintenance of a system?

• Exclusiveness

• A common belief system

- Intolerance of nonmembers
- Designated leaders
- The maintenance of the illusion that the leader loves all members equally.

Magical Processes and the Unconscious in Religious Systems

Magical processes utilized in congregational decision making collude with similarly unrealistic misperceptions of the clergy. By means of magical or distorted thinking, congregations avoid the responsibility for work. Clergy, similarly influenced by tribal magic, develop and maintain a neurotic professional style.

No one is immune from the infectiousness of group membership. The individual feels strong emotional ties to the system and finds it more difficult to remain separate. In a group, then, individual differences tend to disappear. The system itself becomes a substitute superego or conscience. This frees the members from the constraints normally exercised individually through repression. Absence of repression makes acting out more likely because the control for behavior has been shifted from the individual to the system. The system controls acting out by structure, not by conscience. The more structured the system, the greater the control of the unconscious.

Identification with the group, becoming one with it, is enhanced when the identification is focused on a leader or initiator of status. This identification or attachment is often erotic or sensual. When a leader rejects the fantasy love of a member it can be felt deeply. An elevated sensual tie can also increase the likelihood of aggressive acting out.

Membership involves regression. Regression is backward development, reverting to an earlier developmental stage. It is the psychological return to a stage when one felt safe, because one does not feel safe in the present. In most cases the regression is to infancy, a time of physical safety and lower anxiety. The regression that comes with membership in a group or system particularly minimizes anxiety, for there is always safety in numbers and protection in a crowd. When the substitute superego or conscience resides in the group, members are released to operate with less intellectual efficiency, so that regression occurs. Religious leaders often say that they are surprised that bright people can seem stupid when they are working at some religious group function. Even very competent professionals who are members of religious systems cannot draw on their own resources when confronted with a problem within the system. They become like very young children, quick to love and quick to express displeasure or anger when their needs are not being met. They are also often helpless to solve their own problems or work on solutions. Members operate almost purely on primitive emotion.

Like individuals who have regressed, group members experience heightened emotions and intensified emotional expression while their intellect is hampered and inhibited. The religious leader who joins them in their regressed state is also a part of the system and experiences the same regression. No matter what the strength of the group, transference issues are at play. The past of individual members flies or creeps into the present, and along with it comes issues involving authority and the relocating of parental authority with the leader. Transference is unconscious and manifested only in behaviors and not in cognitions (Rioch 1975, 159–77).

Collusion to Work and Collusion to Not-work

Groups rely heavily on symbolism. For example, a religious system looks to its rituals as important glue for its life together. The unconscious life of individuals has been extensively explored, but less attention has been paid to the unconscious life of groups and systems. The most succinct theoretical construct describing the unconscious workings of a group is that of Wilfred Bion (1984). The relationships between religious leader and congregation provide illustrations of these concepts. Bion's key concepts are:

- A group is a phenomenon that is more than a collection of individuals. Therefore, a group exists as an entity.

- The belief system of groups is different from the belief systems of the individuals involved. A system has its own beliefs to which members subscribe in degrees, depending upon the intensity of emotion attached to the joining. The intensity of the born-again experience of fundamentalists, for example, suggests that these persons individually subscribe to the belief system of the fundamentalist group to a greater degree than one might find in group identification within mainstream religious systems.

A group is involved in *working* (a conscious operation) and *not working* (an unconsciously driven operation) at the same time. It is simultaneously aware of and unaware of what it is doing. There is activity in nonwork but it is not directed toward any reality-based task. Three nonwork postures are defined: dependency, fight/flight, and pairing. Bion believes that these postures reflect the unconscious hopes and desires of the group. At any time in the life of a group, some sort of balance between work and nonwork is maintained. There is seldom a time when a system is completely not working. Bion has named these nonwork positions *Basic Assumptions groups,* as each one has a basic assumption on which it bases its irrational and emotional activity. Differences between work and nonwork groups are metaphorical constructs. Metaphors point to the truth but are not identical with it.

Bion's model has been applied in a variety of business, educational, and medical systems, but not to religious ones. This is somewhat surprising, as a religious system is perhaps more susceptible than others to the effects of unconscious function such as we see in the three Basic Assumptions groups. Religious systems are also singularly possessed of the primitive, the magical, and the mysterious.

Each of the three Basic Assumption groups shares characteristics with the others. First, each is in a state of emotional regression in which the intellectual function of the members is inhibited. Second, in each the group behaves as if it believed certain things to be true when they are not. Third, each resists functioning in a rational way to accomplish reasonable ends. The group is convinced of its own version of reality and cannot see or be convinced of any other. As with all defenses, each of the three Basic Assumption group positions functions as an escape from any activity that might result in change. Fourth, as in any other unconsciously driven activity, there is confusion and disorientation as to time, place, and history. As a product of the unconscious, the basic assumption position is manifested behaviorally and shows a total lack of awareness of its own position. Finally, the basic assumption position is strengthened by having become a shared fantasy, and as such it is unaware of the infantile aspects of the relationships within the group. In summary, then, the Basic Assumptions group is primarily irrational and oriented to fantasy and/or magic. It is oriented to past and/or future but not to present. It is also infantile, intolerant, and unlikely to solve its own problems. Characteristically a group will push for a solution external to itself or for a person to solve its problems. Anyone who has worked with religious systems in difficulty will recognize that elements of the Basic Assumptions group are characteristic of a threatened religious system.

The basic assumption of the first nonwork posture, the dependency group, is that the leader will protect them and keep them safe. This group lives through its leader whom they view as omnipotent, the source of all wisdom and comfort. Belief in this leader is a matter of faith. Members present themselves as immature and inadequate, powerless without a leader and important in the hierarchy only when close to the leader.

Since little independent relationship exists between members, group members are jealous, greedy, demanding, and resentful over each other's place in the hierarchy with respect to the leader. When the leader inevitably fails to meet the expectations of the group, resentment turns to hurt and then to aggression.

A fight/flight group sees its primary task as the preservation of the group through some sort of action. There is little tolerance for sickness or weakness of any kind in such a group. This group will quickly expel the sick and the weak. Much scapegoating occurs, and leaders who do not watch their backs are also often attacked. Again, the leader is very important to this group because the leader initiates the call to action. A group expressing the fight/flight basic assumption is anti-intellectual, nonintrospective, and resistant to insight. Any leader who can rally the group against a common enemy is quickly chosen, even at the cost of the former leader who is quickly shunned. This is a hostile and violent group which uses shunning, expulsion, exclusion, and ignoring as more civilized equivalents of killing, banishing, or assassination.

Intervening with a congregational system based in a fight/flight assumption is a dangerous assignment. Those who attempt to be reasonable or to work cooperatively are setting themselves up to become the focus of the group's hatred. This group is struggling to survive, and the act of fearful fight or flight is essential to its very nature. If a leader can harness the fight/flight energy for a legitimate task, the energy can be quite productive. Some urban congregations based in the fight/flight assumption have used the stance as a survival tactic. The angry energy generated by threatened death results in short spurts of hard work. Most such groups, however, do not survive and perhaps should not survive beyond their original limited purpose. The survival fantasy, however, is strong because personal survival is linked to the group's survival. It has been said that the easiest thing in the world to do is to start something, and the hardest is to stop it. Members believe that if the group dies, they will die too.

Mergers between religious institutions often manifest the fight/flight defensive stance in interesting ways. Just as the children of divorce have trouble establishing permanent relationships of their own or else fight for their relationships even when they are in extreme difficulty or beyond repair, so new congregations formed from other groups who have fought for survival and lost will cleave fiercely to the new association, however inappropriate such tenacity may be. In any association threatened with closing, members see their own impending deaths and react accordingly.

The pairing group is a different variation but with a basis just as lacking in realism. It is incredibly hopeful and optimistic that a new idea or person will emerge and extricate the group from their present frustration and dilemma. The pairing group phenomenon is a defensive replication of the messiah wish. Two people, one of whom is usually a leader, get together for the good of the whole. Something or someone who will save the group is expected to emerge from this pairing. Pairing is a sexually charged scenario regardless of the gender of the pair. The group believes that the pairing will have a positive effect on the life of the whole group. At the start of the pairing process, members relate to one another with a utopian enthusiasm and focus their conversation and attention on the pair.

As with stances of the dependency group, this utopian stance of the pairing defense as they lose equilibrium will be maintained only as long as there is no real action but only the promise of change. Should a messiah or life-changing idea actually emerge, it will certainly be rejected or killed, since complete or final solutions exist only in fantasy. In reality all solutions are temporary and are gradually replaced by new problems, frustrations, and tensions. Pairing cultures cannot cope with reality; they want utopia.

Pairing may occur in congregations in which a new leader is to be hired, but it can also arise when a congregation pairs a new staff person with an existing loved leader. Religious professionals also experience quasi-sexual pairing fantasies when taking up new positions or hiring a new staff person.

Valency, another concept used by Wilfred Bion, refers to the degree to which individuals can attach themselves to the group in any one of the three basic assumptions—dependency, fight/flight, or pairing. It is the readiness to enter into and become part of a group. All persons have some degree of valency, but there is a range of high to low. A person who has a fear of joining and perceives this as life-threatening will have low valency, and a person who believes that joining is the essence of life itself will have high valency. Women tend to have higher valency than do men.

The personality structures of individuals determine to some extent their susceptibility to different basic assumptions and the stances they yield. For example, a dependent person is more likely to join with the dependency group than with a fight/flight or pairing group, while a more individualistic or antagonistic person is more likely to join with a fight/flight fantasy. Persons who are more sensually focused will join with the utopian pairing fantasy.

So far, in discussing Bion's typology we have been focusing on nonwork stances of three types. By nonwork we mean activity that is generally unproductive of change within a system. Dependency, fight/flight, and pairing fantasies posit an everlasting status quo arrived at through magic and maintained through fantasy. Nonwork stances can exist only as long as nothing changes within a system.

Both work and nonwork phases are essential to a system, but work phases differ markedly from nonwork. Instead of generating unproductive anxiety and unusable energy, work groups require the use of energy, are based on realistic assessment, are maintained only with great effort, and are directed toward change of the system. They depend on conscious rather than unconscious impulses that drive effective work rather than fueling self-depriving fantasy.

There is a parallel between a group's behavior as it moves toward change and an individual patient's behavior in therapy. The more effective the interpretations of the unconscious become, the more mature the patient. The more centered on conscious work phases rather than unconscious nonwork phases, the more healthy the group. It is important, therefore, to render conscious within a group those impulses that have stayed below the surface in nonwork phases.

The membership's love for a caring leader as manifested in a dependency culture may be useful for a period of time in a healthy community that needs to bond with a new leader. The energy of the fight/flight group against a legitimate common enemy may also be useful. Utopian visions provide a glimpse of the ideal to which the actual can strive. Either ignoring the unconscious workings of a group or misunderstanding the limitations of its basic assumptions can, however, lead to disastrous results.

When a group refuses to accept personal responsibility and resists work, it is probably manifesting a defensive fantasy stance that is blocking its progress, just as resistance blocks the progress of an individual who is in therapy and moving toward maturity.

There is a circular flow from one fantasy position to another and back again to the beginning. The hope for the new idea, the new direction, the new leader/messiah (pairing) gives way to the belief in an omnipotent and protecting leader (dependent), and then, when the leader fails to meet the needs of the membership, the group yields to anger and hostility against the leader (fight/flight) and hence back to the unrealistic search for a new leader.

Look at the process within the context of a religious group. A hypothetical congregation is without a leader. The congregational members tend to feel helpless. They exert pressure on the search committee, or the call committee, or the hiring committee, or the judiciary executives to send them a leader. What they really want is a messiah, someone who will lead them back into the fantasy of past glory or on to future glory.

The congregation is in the dependency basic assumption group phase. The congregation stands ready to pledge love and enduring support to almost any leader who comes to them, and the members are willing to support the final choice overwhelmingly and irrationally. They declare their need to be loved and cared for. They promise endless love.

All religious professionals know about the honeymoon period of a new position. Few are naïve enough to believe the line that was handed to them at the hiring. Nevertheless, religious professionals want very much to believe they are loved, and for a period of time they are able to revel in it.

The basic assumption of the dependency group is that members feel secure and protected by the leader. They present themselves as powerless, immature, and inadequate, trusting the leader's omnipotence.

The honeymoon period continues as long as no one, especially the new leader, does anything. Lack of action cannot extend the period of dependency indefinitely, however. Fantasy/magic positions are devoid of the kind of energy that moves a system forward. They exist on pure emotion. As soon as any action begins, the fantasy position begins to shift to the fight/flight assumption. When the leader inevitably fails to meet the dependency expectations of the membership, resentment and anger emerge which may result in the aggression of the fight/flight mode.

In the work position or the work group, as contrasted with the basic assumption groups, a congregation or part of one is very much oriented in the present. There is a sense of time, place, and history. Work is contextual and involves understanding. In the work mode the congregation has the ability to be reasonable, rational, and logical; it can plan, set goals, and act in terms of present needs, not unrealistic future goals or past patterns. According to Bion, however, most systems are operating in an unrealistic unconsciously driven mode about 80 percent of the time. Little wonder that so little work is actually done in systems.

It is also important to recall and acknowledge that the very same congregation that succeeds in rational organization and work also operates in an emotionally regressed manner. Take, for example, a medium-sized midwestern congregation consisting of male and female high-level, bright executives, attorneys, teachers, and other professionals. These are upper-middle-class people who are capable, competent, well educated, successful, and very committed to their faith and the work of that congregation.

As individuals these people seem to function well at work, but when they enter the church something magical happens. They cannot think. They are confused and frustrated. As a group these people feel absolutely incapable of deciding anything for themselves. They ask for outside assistance and get it from their bishop's office. The recommendations of the bishop are, in fact, the same kinds of decisions that these very members make individually and regularly in their workplaces.

Why did the members not function as well in the congregation? The answer lies in the strength of the people's commitment to their congregation and the emotionally regressed position imposed by the group on some of the high-valency members of the system. Even here, however, there were a few low-valency thinking people who were able to participate in the solution. The division of time spent in work and nonwork was consistent with Bion's theory. About 80 percent of a system's energy is spent in an unconsciously driven regression, while 20 percent is spent in a reality orientation.

How does the group move into and out of the fantasy/magic position? This has much to do with valency. A person with high valency is more susceptible to regression and to the fantasy/magic posture when in a group. The person who has low valency or low susceptibility is less likely to join, or, having joined, maintains a more independent sense of reality. In some places such persons are viewed as oppositional. Since most persons have high valency, and those longest attached to a group are apt to be most involved with it, a high proportion of leadership and membership operate from the fantasy/magic position. They have long since overcome the threat and pain of loss of individuality.

As the fantasy/magic continues, the third assumption emerges. Either the congregation looks for a helper to pair with the fallen leader to achieve a new messiah, or it attempts to pair itself symbolically with a new leader once the original one has been disposed of. In one case I observed, a group paired an old leader who had lost credibility with a study document proposing radical structural changes. As the deficiencies of the structural change proposal were exposed, the possibility of pairing this structure with the old leader diminished and a general malaise infused the total system. As there was no hope for change from the fantasy pairing, the system exhibited symptoms of a groupwide depression. When pairing actually does take place, the assumption position transforms itself once more into dependency. Once again, the interconnectedness of depression and dependency can be seen.

How can work be accomplished in the midst of so much dysfunctional defensiveness and belligerent regression? How can a religious professional function with any effectiveness? In most religious systems there remain islands of clarity. Work can be happening for about 10 to 15 percent of the congregation or religious system at any point in time, regardless of the unconscious life that goes on simultaneously.

In order for the religious system to work as a whole, it is essential that the workers and especially the professional leader understand the nature of the unconscious assumptions of the majority that seem to be preventing the system from moving forward. If they understand the dynamics of the majority, they can sometimes harness its unproductive energy and make it productive. More often, by understanding the seriousness of the block to conscious action, the minority can work around it.

Does work occur at the committee meeting, or does it take place in the diner over coffee among the four committee members who remained behind and who really cared about the projects? The situation of a religious system differs little from a corporation or school in this respect. The work of a corporation seldom happens regularly between 8:30 A.M. and 4:30 P.M. It happens more often over the telephone late at night, in informal conversation in the cafeteria, or in the parking lot on the way home. Learning seldom happens in the class time, but more often takes place upon reflection after class, alone in the library, or in a conversation with a teacher or a friend. The structured times formerly designated as working hours are often times of fantasy and magic provoked by the rituals to which we submit.

The work posture is identifiable by what is present when it is taking place. It is associated with an absence of authority problems and a clear consciousness of tasks to be accomplished. There are clear and realistic limits both to the task and to the powers of those responsible for it. A work group knows that there is a beginning and an end to the task. It can reflect and be perceptive. The work group is conscious of its own process; it knows when it is working and when it is not working. In a work group, bright people can contribute from their own resources and appreciate the resources of others in the group. The work group tolerates differences.

Religious leaders need to understand defensive postures, to be conscious of their own issues, and to ensure that they are maturely grounded in reality.

Mature and Immature Leadership

According to Fritz Redl (1980, 15–71) an immature leader is one who uses the leadership position primarily as a means of satisfying personal needs rather than the needs of the group. Eventually immature leadership fosters immature participation. It is possible, therefore, for a congregational system to change over time from a well-directed one to an immature one under the leadership of an immature religious professional.

Gradually the change is accompanied by the withdrawal or the decreased activity of the more mature members. An unfortunate effect of immature leadership is that immaturity accentuates an individual's drive to lead, so that an immature leader is likely to become a leader several times. Those who follow the tenure of an immature leader are entering immature and regressed systems, which are operating in one of the basic assumption postures. The first task of the new leader is to encourage the reentry of those members who withdrew earlier and who will best help to lead the group back to reality.

Redl further defines the characteristics of a mature leader as one who is able to determine the climate of the system. That is, a leader must have an ability not only to determine the basic assumption postures of a group but also to sense the basic feeling tone or climate that underlies the life of the group. A system can have one of three primary climates: the punitive climate, the emotional blackmail climate, and the group pride climate. A group with a punitive climate seeks members, or more probably outsiders, to punish for what they consider to be behavior contrary to group interest. In an emotional blackmail climate, less fervent members and all nonmembers are made to feel guilt and shame for their lack of fervor. The group pride climate affirms the group as a good thing without diverting energy toward either ranking its members or criticizing outsiders.

A climate will only change over time with mature leadership. A congregation's attitude toward a leader is determined by the leader's ability to meet the basic needs of the membership and by the strength of the emotional attachment to the leader. A mature leader is sensitive to the needs of the members, able and willing to give and take emotionally, and relatively free from unconscious conflicts.

To be a good leader, the religious professional must pay close attention to personal issues; otherwise, the leader will never meet the needs of the group in a mature way. Since a group's unconscious is often more powerful than the unconscious of the individuals who compromise the group, the new leader needs to add a strong and shaping conscious to the mix. It is essential that the leader have the self-knowledge to contribute to, and not be overwhelmed or seduced by, that powerful group unconscious.

MARRIAGE: THE OTHER SYSTEM

There is not much that is mysterious or magical about marriage. Marriage is a relatively simple process about which much is predictable and much dysfunctional. Any culture that uses romantic love as the criterion for marriage partner selection will have dysfunctional marriages among all groups in the culture, including religious professionals. Love and choice of marriage partner involves a combination of proximity, chemistry, and pathology. The two individuals, while convinced that they have made the right choice, are wrong at least half the time. When making a second marriage choice, the partners are wrong about two out of three times. A record that bad cannot be a matter of chance alone. The odds would be better for a single heterosexual female to ask every man she met to marry her until one said yes. If neither had been married before, a marriage begun this way would have the same chance of succeeding as the average marriage between another couple who engaged in the entire cultural ritual that begins with falling in love.

Romantic love had its beginnings in the twelfth century but came to full flower in the seventeenth century. This eroticized process later became a criterion for life-long choice-making in relationships. Originally, it was meant as an exciting and sometimes illicitly dangerous way to pass the time, not as a prelude to marriage. From its beginnings, romantic love was a concept applied to extramarital involvements. Courtiers knew that being *in love* is among the most emotionally charged and exciting of human experiences. Fortunately for them and for us, it does not last for long periods of time. Our physical and emotional systems simply cannot sustain the energy necessary for romantic love.

Somewhat later, romantic love emerged as an expected preliminary to marriage in Western culture and replaced family arrangements for property exchange. Romantic love altered and confused the character of long-term relationships. It further altered the concept of love. Falling in love works less well as a preparation for marriage than did family negotiating. One reason for this is that the basis for negotiated marriages was relative economic status; psychological pathologies were not being unconsciously matched in these arranged marriages.

Marriage began as a social contract for forming family units and was designed to make life more bearable and less chaotic. Its roots were in social control and economics. Marriage provided a social structure and was never intended primarily as a structure for meeting emotional needs. As the demand for meeting emotional needs increased during the last third of the twentieth century, the institution has come under increased threat.

Many contexts and many separate persons apart from marriage contribute to meeting our emotional needs. To overload the limits of marriage with demands that it satisfy all our needs is to endanger it.

The process seems deceptively simple: Fall in love and get married while relatively young, and then spend the rest of your adult life trying to believe that the choice you made was the right one. Perhaps for those who are young, this process appeals to a seemingly clear, undistorted vision.

It is not the idea of marriage that is wrong, but the distortions within ourselves that we bring to the process, as well as our unconscious selves that interfere with our choice making. Falling in love triggers all sorts of neurotic and unconsciously driven impulses in people. For example, a person with damaged self-esteem often falls in love with someone she believes to think well of himself, only to discover that he also has damaged self-esteem. People most often fall in love with those who appear to have solved all the personal issues with which they themselves are plagued. Thus it is not opposites but the perception of an opposite that attracts. Why do so many of the abused fall in love with abusers? Why do narcissists so frequently fall in love with depressed/dependent persons? Why do compulsives often find each other and compulsively declare their relationship to be for life? Love appears to have its origins more in pathology than in maturity.

Defensive structures and early development are intimately involved in the business of falling in love. While it may seem too cynical to call falling in love the finding of matching pathologies, there is some truth in this definition. Since only three major defensive structures are manifested among immature professionals, these persons have available to them only a few possible variations to choose from in a marriage partner.

It was once suggested that all persons should marry twice: the first time for growing up and the second for childbearing and the rest of life. This seldom happens in so rational an order. Pat and Salvador Minuchin, pioneers in family therapy, have been married for over forty years. They have said that their long marriage had less to do with hard work than with luck. As they grew individually, they did not grow far apart. They emphasize that their marriage should not be taken as a model. Successful and long-term marriages can be thought of as not one but several marriages to the same person in more or less maturational sequence.

Other factors interfere with or diminish the possibility of life-long marriage relationships. Our longevity is one of them. Touring old cemeteries serves as a reminder of the long-lived husband and several younger wives a century or so ago; when women's lives were often shortened by the ravages of hard physical work and painful childbirth, a life-long marriage was not all that long. Even a short time ago, a fiftieth wedding anniversary was an event worthy of a photograph in the local newspaper. Now these events are commonplace. The concept of life-long marriage further fails to take into account the fact that in former days men and often women had more than one relationship, one for procreation and the other for sexual pleasure. Life-long marriage seems much more difficult to maintain when life itself is much longer and the expectations are so much greater.

The social acceptance of divorce in our present culture poses yet another threat to the marital institution, even though depressed economies appear to impede divorce. Divorce is a very old way out of unhealthy relationships, but the assumption or hope that it would lead to a new beginning in life has, for the most part, wreaked havoc rather than shed grace. Increasing seriousness about making marriages work through premarital counseling; waiting to marry until one is more mature; living together before marriage; becoming better informed about marital issues—none of these has altered marital statistics in any way. The failure rate for first marriages hovers consistently around fifty percent.

No human being can be intellectually exciting, caring, supportive and nurturing, strong and dependable, good at practical tasks and organization, sexually appealing, and emotionally available all the time. While people can acknowlege this on a rational level, more often than not they continue to accept the myth that a marriage partner will make up for all the damage they received from imperfect parents. Both sexes are often desperate to rejoin with a fantasy mother or father. In religious persons some of this fantasy expectation is projected onto God, but not even God can bear the weight of the fantasy, so the marriage partner pays the price. The expectations of both sexes are similar in many ways, with biology responsible for minor differences.

Romantic love also involves considerable lust. Rollo May once wrote:

> A common practice in our day is to avoid working up the courage required for authentic intimacy by shifting the issue to the body. . . . It is easier in our society to be naked physically than naked psychologically or spiritually—easier to share our body than to share our fantasies, hopes, fears and aspirations, which are felt to be more personal. . . . After all, the body is an object and can be treated mechanically. (1975, 18)

Lust is not passion. Passion runs far deeper. Once a physical interaction begins, a couple can learn if their relationship is about passion or just about lust. If the relationship is about lust, then, when the couple abstains from the physical, the unassuaged hunger often becomes a larger and larger part of the relationship and distorts the partners' reality, thus interfering with addressing other, more important issues.

Physical lust complicates marriages by overloading expectations and becoming confused with love. Males expect their spouses to be sexually exciting all the time, even when they are sexually inhibited themselves.

Women want their partners to relate to them as if they are whole and worthwhile persons, not some disembodied combination of three body parts. If sex is a gift of the Creator, it is certainly the most confounding and confusing one offered.

Personality Structure and Partner Selection

The at-risk religious professional can engage only in limited kinds of marital relationships, since one at-risk person can only fall in love with another at-risk person. Narcissists choose depressed/dependent partners who adore them and stay loyal in spite of the narcissist's frenetic behavior. The compulsive will fall in love with another compulsive. The depressed/ dependent will fall in love with a narcissist more often than with another depressed/dependent. When two depressed/dependents are mutually attracted, the weight of the dependency usually keeps the relationship from lasting into marriage. There are few variants. The professional who combines narcissism and compulsivity will almost always choose a depressed/ dependent person with a strong compulsive back-up defense. A narcissistic patient recently came to realize that one criterion for deciding if a relationship was going to be unhealthy was simply whether there was mutual attraction. As he is becoming aware of the severity of his own dysfunction he realizes that any woman who finds him attractive and wants to pursue a relationship is almost certainly the wrong person for a relationship.

In all cases, when one immature partner begins to mature, the relationship is in trouble. When the depressed/dependent becomes assertive or more independent, the narcissist may act out disagreeably or move on to another lover or another place. Often the depressed/dependent person must travel the painful route of past abuses, abandonments, or victimizations to move toward independence. Being abandoned by the current narcissistic partner does not help.

Dysfunctional marriages are not the coming together of two whole selves but the merger of two parts into a single ego. Unresolved separation issues contribute to making the couple into a two-headed, four-legged creature. Neither person can continue without the other, although each pretends otherwise. This is pseudo-separation and it is seductive. The couple is seduced by their own pretend separateness. At first, the supposed togetherness may seem like a good thing. Each partner supports the other in the accomplishment of career goals or the more mundane tasks about the home. As a team the couple moves from one life task to the next: decorating the first apartment, selecting furniture and paying for it, buying a first house, having and raising children, working for promotions to pay off the new debt. All these tasks keep the marriage going, and neither raises any important questions about the relationship. If questions exist, they are kept secret. This process is task focus, not intimacy.

Intimacy requires separateness, which the task-focused couple does not have and cannot have without maturing. When couples have trouble working together, or when this step-by-step movement is interrupted or inhibited, the important questions arise more quickly. This happens, for example, when a problem of infertility must be faced or a major accident or other catastrophe occurs. But when major trauma leads to increasing maturity, the marriage is at risk. Little wonder that the divorce rate for couples who have experienced a major trauma is 80 percent rather than the cultural average of 50 percent.

Breakdown of At-risk Marriages

How do marriages between at-risk people break down? If the partners begin to mature, real separation begins. The narcissist begins to see himself as human and limited. The need for adoration slows and a peer interaction with his partner can begin. The narcissist, of course, was always certain that it was the depressed/dependent partner who caused the problems in the marriage. The depressed/dependent partner yields to the pressure of the narcissist and pursues a program of counseling. The newly maturing partner is no longer willing to be the adoring and supporting one. Mature persons do not choose to stay in relationships with narcissists for long. These changing marriages are at risk.

As compulsives begin to mature, they discover and begin to enjoy spontaneity in the life process. As they further awaken, they even discover their passion. At the same time, they become aware of how predictable, joyless, and emotionally constricted their partner may be. Such a relationship is also at risk.

The implication is clear: The marital structure itself is often part of the cost of maturing. A psychologist or counselor can quickly assess the prognosis for a troubled relationship. For example, when one party openly addresses the problems in the relationship while the other party holds one foot firmly on the emotional brake, the prognosis is not good. This does not inevitably lead to the end of the relationship, as many unhealthy relationships continue for long periods of time. High levels of empathy coupled with genuine caring for the other bodes well for a positive outcome.

10

TRANSFERENCE AND COUNTERTRANSFERENCE

One source of acting out (or its reverse, acting in) must be given what may seem to be disproportionate treatment. The reason for this is that the inappropriate behavior will be observed in a context that is almost unique to the situation of the religious professional as he or she deals therapeutically with the problems of damaged congregational members.

When this acting out occurs, as it does with greater frequency than once believed, it is the chief cause of removal from the religious professions, and it causes great pain not only to the professionals themselves but also to the very people they would be serving. There is also evidence that acting out of this sort in the therapeutic context can damage an entire congregation or religious community. Acting in in response to this particular threat of loss of control may also result in loss of position or breakdown.

First let us look closely at the dynamics of the relationship within which acting out may occur and, as we do this, at the manner in which things may go wrong. This is the phenomenon of transference and countertransference. These terms originated as specialized psychoanalytic concepts. Transference is generally deemed essential to analytic healing, and many believe that countertransference inevitably accompanies it. If inappropriately used, these two processes can also cause failures in relationships between professionals and the people they would help, most frequently by resulting in either sexual or destructive though immaculate affairs. The immaculate affair (an intimate, though not sexual affair) is the most frequent acting-out phenomenon among religious professionals in mainline denominations. The most common acting-in phenomenon may also result from transference gone awry. It is professional burnout or depression.

Transference has always been perceived as both benefit and curse. Positive transference is necessary to the helping process. In the presence

135

of a person who is both supportive and nonthreatening, one can most easily work through the painful material of one's past. The presence of the neutral, unjudging spectator to self-discovery allows the painful material to surface in a useful way that connects past to present positively. Since the material of the past is so emotionally laden, however, part of the released emotion often attaches to the one with whom the revivified past is being shared. It is at this stage of the helping process that the helper becomes most at risk. Being present at the rediscovery of the blocked painful past is a little like being present, and unable to escape, at the splitting of an atom. An immature helper is most likely to become trapped in an emotional net and to lose all ability to help.

The helper's conscious and unconscious reaction to the new emotional bond formed with the one being helped is called countertransference. Traditionally, any countertransference was considered to signify immaturity and almost guaranteed to have a negative effect on the healing process. Therapists were trained to avoid it at any cost. However, Otto Kernberg ([1981] 1990, 207–14) assesses countertransference more realistically, defining it as the total emotional reaction felt by the helper toward the client in treatment. According to this definition, the therapist reacts to the patient's reality as well as to the transference that the patient accords the helper. On the other hand, the reality and the distortions of the therapist also come into play. To prepare oneself to be a therapist, one needs to resolve and remove as many of one's own distortions as possible. This is done through a program of personal psychodynamic therapy as part of professional preparation. But even with a successful program of therapy one is left incomplete and less mature at some levels than at others. Once professional helpers become self-conscious about their own distortions and learn that these reactions are important, these can help in understanding the dynamics of the therapeutic relationships in which they are involved. Transference and countertransference thus become part of interpersonal interaction. If a relationship with a client or a congregational member generates ambivalent emotion, this is not in itself bad. It can be a useful adjunct to the helping role.

Transference is ubiquitous. It is happening all the time and in virtually every setting. Countertransference is the other person's reaction to transference. One of my former supervisors liked to illustrate the two powerful processes with this anecdote. She said, "I look into the mirror every morning and I see myself. I know what I look like and who I am. When a patient begins to relate to me in ways contrary to that which I see in the morning, that is transference. When the patient begins to look different to me, more desirable, more repulsive or more like my brother, that is countertransference."

TRANSFERENCE WHEN CLERGY
ARE HELPERS

In this context I am reminded that while clergy serve as healers, they are, like everyone else in this world, themselves people in need and in process of healing. As they seek the missing pieces of themselves and try to understand the wounds of their past before these become transmogrified into the wounds of the present, they must realize that they are doing this in the presence of other wounded people of their own sort. They should seek to complete themselves without wounding others who trust and need them.

Harold Searles ([1981] 1990, 103–34) has written about a seemingly basic human need to be psychologically or therapeutically helpful to others. Clergy have the opportunity to meet this need as few others do. How often has the motivation for entry into the ecclesiastical profession been described in these very terms? Candidates often cite their desire to help people as primary. The problems occur when helping others is primarily motivated by the need for self importance or self-fulfillment that comes through quasi-messianic means. When professionals see themselves as the wizards, the focus is on the helper and not the other needing help. Under these circumstances the needs of the congregational member primarily serve the needs of the professional.

Even though both terms could be used multidirectionally, transference being the action and countertransference being the reaction, I will consider the actions of congregational members, marriage partners, or peers to be transference and the reaction of the clergy or helper to be countertransference. Both action and reaction are rooted in material from our past. Both represent a distortion of reality, a departure from the here and now. The past flies into the present and overwhelms it so that the present is only a repetition of some usually incomplete past relationship.

What is peculiar to the religious community as the locus of therapeutic healing? Just as the person seeking help of a minister, rabbi, or religious institution-based counselor is trying to deal with some past pain experienced in a family setting, so the very language of religious settings reflects a family and familiar analogy: mother, father, sister, rabbi, children of God. When a person in need of help seeks the approval of a priest, pastor, or rabbi, almost inevitably that person is covertly seeking the approval of a long-ago father or mother. By the very station he or she occupies, the religious professional is not allowed to maintain a neutral role as required in therapy, but instead must occupy a role of authority, adorned and codified by vestments, rituals, and sanctified titles. There is nothing neutral about the presence of the clergy or clergy family in the congregation. Friendships formed with members of the clergy family in the parish permit a few to have even closer relationships to clergy who presumably serve them. Despite recent tendencies to remove the clergy from positions of importance in the community and make the church more democratic, the clergy have not been moved to a position of neutrality. Clergy remain in the center and represent complete sets of expectations for each member of the parish. This makes the transference phenomenon more charged than any that occurs in the therapist's office. The role itself speeds and exaggerates transference.

COUNTERTRANSFERENCE AND THE CLERGY

We have already established that many clergy carry much unresolved material into their profession. Therefore the countertransference process between clergy and parishioners becomes more potentially threatening than a similar process between two nonprofessionals.

Human beings need human contact, and church work done in common builds bonds between clergy and parishioners. The base for maturity is established, first by sensory contact with mother and later through connection with others. Connections to the whole creation cannot exist without beginning with connections to our own kind. The roots of the transference phenomenon are therefore very basic and very primitive. Transference involves an unconscious connection with the other as if the other were mother or father. Loving feelings, and angry ones as well, are directed toward the object of the transference. To be certain, clergy have their own transference relationships with members, regularly projecting their pasts onto the present as it is found in new relationships.

In transference, the relationship quickly moves to one of liking or of enmity. Once the emotional bond is formed, the transference/countertransference process begins and it can move very quickly. William Lederer and Don Jackson (1968, 132–34) referred to relationships such as those between clergy and parishioners that begin around a common task as "heavenly twins" relationships. A commitment to a common project becomes the focus, and the similarities of the two persons involved become exaggerated as they combine into a whole. Once the action/reaction process, which merges into a simultaneous dance, has begun, the parties are beyond reach. Little wonder that Irvin Yalum titled a recent book *Love's Executioner* (1989). It is a work which, in part, describes the impossibility of intervention in the life of a patient who is in love. No one can reach the two who have become entangled. Both have become anesthetized against reality. This tyranny of infatuation is common in clergy-parishioner affairs, which often start with unintentioned transference followed by countertransference, followed by a total loss of separateness, followed by a loss of the ability to help or be helped.

Transference and countertransference are unconscious processes. Both are potentially dangerous and potentially helpful to each party. Transference can help a patient reestablish where he or she is. If it is to work this way, however, the helper must strive for as much neutrality as possible, or at least must know just where he or she fits in, so that the process of transference itself can be first encouraged and then interpreted for the patient as part of the journey from unconsciousness to consciousness.

Relating through transference and countertransference is basically very primitive. It is loaded with ambivalent, sexual, and aggressive material. Every congregation has both immature and mature members. The mature church professional knows the difference between them and is able to respond to them accordingly.

For less mature or at-risk clergy, a mixed congregational membership is itself a risk. Some members threaten and are perceived to be attacking. Some members seem to manifest love for the clergy and are perceived as safe and supportive. Some members are perceived to adore the clergy and elicit grandiose responses. Countertransference reactions abound. Even if the professional never acts out openly and never becomes depressed, the reactions are there. Given enough years, a congregation with one at-risk leader will tend to retain as an active membership mainly those members who elicit nondestructive countertransference reactions. Those members who do not respond as the professional wishes will shrink to inactivity or into fringe activities. They may move to another congregation. Often a conflict develops between the clergyperson and the congregation, which is really a pathological struggle involving unconscious power and aggression issues, which neither clergy nor members are able or willing to address.

First Countertransference Problem: Regression

Countertransference is most likely to be a problem when it happens early in a relationship with a client or congregational member and when the emotional reaction is intense. This early, quick, and strong reaction is threatening to any useful clergy-member interaction.

Maturity and immaturity are not either/or polarities. There are degrees of each. The degree of immaturity correlates with the degree to which a professional helper is at risk. Therefore, the greater the degree of immaturity or damage, the greater the depth of unresolved needs and the more powerful and potentially problematic the countertransference reactions.

There are two countertransference reactions that are problematic for the at-risk helper. The first is *regression*.

The root of transference and countertransference is a primitive reenactment of an early developmental scene between parent and child in the hope that it will work out differently this time. This cannot work out, however, because the helper, too, is damaged and has regressed. He or she becomes a false and failed parent in the new relationship. The incestuous abuse is repeated, leaving the victim with one more experience of victimization to add to the accumulated record. This most serious professional breach as a result of individual pathology does not respond to treatment except with years of psychodynamic therapy. Often the abuser is the product of abuse in his or her own development.

The same processes can emerge in less obviously damaging manifestations. Take, for example, the case of an immature church professional who wants desperately to be loved by members of the congregation whom he perceives as the ideal family to compensate for his own developmental damage at the hands of his parents. He is easily seduced by the initial warmth and acceptance that accompanies many new beginnings. After a short time, the newness fades. The members begin to present expectations, which they want to have fulfilled. The immature clergyperson regresses to childhood, infantile threat of withdrawn affection, or disapproval analogous to the one that caused childhood wounds. The clergyperson then reacts angrily toward the apparently unfair demands, or with shame at having failed to fulfill expectations. A long-ago drama is reenacted on this new congregational stage. The helping relationship is damaged. Members want their leader to exhibit a maturity of which he or she is incapable, and the helper wants unconditional love, which the members are unable to give. The two damaged states collide, and neither professional nor congregation is able to help the other. The relationship, while not scandalous, is a distorted one involving transference/countertransference issues stemming from unresolved material.

A problematic countertransference reaction characteristic of female therapists, and thus, by extension, one to which female clergy are susceptible, is the desire to nurture the patient in ways that inhibit growth. Female church professionals who perceive their strength to be a nurturing one may experience such reactions. They unconsciously fear that any maturity on the part of the membership is a threat to their own importance as nurturer. The transference/countertransference trap again keeps caregiver and cared-for from mature interaction.

Second Countertransference Problem: Withdrawal

A second problematic countertransference reaction is withdrawal. *Withdrawal* is an emotional move away from involvement with a congregational member; it is a form of passive indifference or inner abandonment. Withdrawal marks the beginning of the end of a relationship because the professional's detachment replaces her empathy, although the actual end may yet be several years in the making. This aspect of withdrawal is not what is meant by professional detachment. Professional detachment is the deliberate achievement of separateness in order to promote individual responsibility for healing. It is not the removal of the emotional self. Removal of self, on the contrary, is a move often taken by those professional helpers who are unconsciously afraid of connections and of the potential power of their own sexual or aggressive tendencies; essentially they are people who do not trust themselves. This detachment usually follows a strong transference action that triggers a quite negative countertransference reaction. The leader or helper begins to perceive the other as personally threatening. Since the leader is indifferent to or has psychologically abandoned the other, the relationship comes to an end. No longer can the leader give help, and no longer can the other person receive help from the leader.

Concern as Golden Mean

These two reactions, the tendency to regress to childhood and the tendency to withdraw, will not just go away. They are chronic reactions and respond only to the maturing facilitated by successful intervention. Otto Kernberg ([1981] 1990, 213–14) suggests an interim measure or a bridging device, which he calls concern. *Concern* is understood as an authentic wish and need to help and not to damage. Sometimes, when empathy or distance are not yet possible, concern will bridge the gap. Even through rather significant negative countertransference reactions, congregational members can be served by the professional who evidences concern alone. Conversely, immature clergy who elicit strong countertransference responses from congregational members can be served by a concerned member when empathy is not possible.

Professional church work is about relationships. It is always about intimate connections—dangerous, powerful, and exhilarating. The ability to empathize is critical for the task but the need to be intimate is not. Separateness can permit empathic response and still keep a safe distance between persons. Only when distance is maintained can the foundations of helping be built. On the other hand, distance without empathy is an empty space.

Effective therapy within religious and other settings requires both distance and empathy. Concern, as defined by Kernberg, can serve as a golden mean between the two; it can act as a thin line between the excessive distance that may result in withdrawal and depression for the professional (acting in) and the excessive involvement that may result in unhealthy countertransference and affairs (acting out). The religious professional is neither a wizard nor a person without resource, neither unique nor unremarkable. The more professionals know and accept themselves, the more they will be able to help others.

WHEN CLERGY
NEED COUNSELING

Clergy have a tendency to perceive themselves as different from other people. This tendency clouds their sensibility in knowing when to seek counseling. When is it time for the clergy to become client?

People change when the energy needed to remain the same can no longer be sustained in the face of external events or circumstances (Weiser 1983). Sometimes these external events and circumstances stretch to the breaking point the person's ability to maintain defenses. Changes, however, do release for other purposes the energies once directed toward maintaining defensive structures.

This conception of energy originates in neurophysiology. The neurons that comprise the central nervous system do not fire gradually or incrementally; a neuron will only fire when enough energy has been accumulated to create the spark. Often it takes several sources of incoming energy to create the condition for the firing of the neuron. In some ways, human beings respond like neurons. While the conditions that require attention may be present for many years, they have to reach a flash point to cause change. In other words, change seems to happen on a kairotic rather than chronological schedule.

THE KEY TO WHOLENESS

Intensive dynamic, individual, long-term psychotherapy—a process that powerfully connects intellectual to emotional content—holds the key to wholeness. A comprehensive dynamic assessment will also be useful for therapist and patient alike. Medication may sometimes also be a useful adjunct to psychotherapy, particularly for depression. Each damaged religious professional requires an intense process of personality restructuring in order to compensate for original developmental damage.

143

When professionals have problems, an inventory in all areas of their lives needs to be taken: marriage, family, collegial relationships, congregation, friendships. The crisis that precipitated the therapy may have originated in one branch of the life only, but the problem is systemic. Injury to other areas may result, and we do not know which other areas are at risk. Nor, hard as that may seem, must we concentrate too much attention on the victims of the immediate crisis or those threatened by future crisis.

The specific fall-out is often staggering, but the problems that precipitated it have been present for a long time in all systems. The immediate and potential damage needs attention, intervention, and treatment but this crisis intervention does not directly contribute to the treatment of the religious professional. Effective treatment for the professional involves weekly (twice weekly is often preferable) psychotherapy sessions often over a period of two to five years. Some low-functioning conditions may require a longer period of treatment, while others may not respond to treatment at all. The motivation and resistance of the patient are important factors here.

In the case of at-risk professionals, prevention is not worth more than cure. Traditional educational programs, in spite of the fact that they are increasingly popular in religious systems and seminaries, will not work because specific damage cannot be addressed by teaching methods alone. Some recent prevention programs have applied the law, that is, attempts to deter by fear and directed prohibition. Simply to order a religious professional not to do certain things will not work. These legalistic processes fail to recognize that many damaged church professionals believe themselves to be unique and therefore not susceptible to the same failings as normal human beings.

An even less popular truth these days is this: There are no short-term interventions able to generate structural change for the dysfunctional religious professional. Our culture has difficulty with the concept of long-term therapy; one need only recall that Americans invented the quick-fix of biofeedback as a substitute for yogic meditation, a technique that takes many years to master. Americans also talk freely about their subconscious but have little understanding of the unconscious. One would hope that religious professionals are not average Americans but intelligent adults willing and able to address the incredible complexity of their own multilayered nature. For accomplishing that and for understanding the rational, the irrational, and the developmental processes within us, there is no better tool than analytic psychology.

The fruits of healing for those who undergo this therapeutic course of treatment will be health and maturity that combine physical, emotional, cognitive, spiritual, theological, psychological, and existential components in such a way that the individual is enabled both to be and to act differently. With the attainment of health and maturity anxiety is lowered and an interaction with life and with others on their own terms is possible. One also learns to live with a consciousness of one's limitations.

TREATMENT OF THE PROFESSIONAL

Religious systems have tended to view acting out episodes as if the action has been under conscious control. In most cases this is not true. This is not to say that at-risk professionals should accept no responsibility for their actions, but only that their at-risk condition resulted from damaged selves of which they were unconscious. They are wounded human beings who are highly neurotic and cognitively rigid, emotionally constricted, or insufficiently constricted. They are not mature enough to have thought through their actions prior to acting out or acting in or to have considered that acting in or acting out was inappropriate.

As many as one-third of professional populations are potential abusers or seducers (narcissist), potential victims or abused (depressed/dependent), or at risk for the potential explosion of severe acting out or for the implosion of depression called burnout (compulsive). In most cases, all three conditions exist in the same person in varying degrees and account for perceptions of difference from person to person.

What is learned from most crises is that one survives them, although for a time death may appear preferable to survival. The crisis becomes an excellent opportunity for religious professionals to grow, but it takes a long time. When defensive structures explode, implode, or disintegrate, the possibility arises, to a greater or lesser extent, of moving from the defensiveness of immaturity to more mature adult functioning.

Conditions at Intervention or Crisis

At-risk professionals do not often know they are in trouble until it is too late. Those able to self-diagnose are already aware of their own issues and mature enough not to be at-risk. The at-risk professional is repressed or in denial and has little awareness of being on the verge of crisis. Most often such a professional resists intervention even by friends, peers, family, or congregational members.

The lower the level of function, the more defensively driven the individual and the greater the likelihood of crisis. Greater stress lowers the level of functioning. Right up to the point of crisis the professional is attempting to shore up defensive structures, and this causes greater stress and more dysfunction.

There are three conditions possible at the time of intervention or a crisis: The defensive structure is still intact; it is disintegrating; or it has already exploded or imploded. When defensive structures are still intact, as in many cases of sexual abusers, treatment is often neither helpful nor effective. Forced resignation for sexual offenses almost always leaves the abusing religious professional with all defenses intact. "I was only trying to help" is their most frequent defense. Sexual offenders are most often low-functioning narcissists with antisocial features. They are usually not treatable, as their defensive structure causes them to externalize responsibility for their actions, justify the actions, or minimize their importance. Among religious professionals treatment is most difficult for narcissistic and borderline conditions, as it is in any other population.

When defensive structures are breaking down or have already collapsed, wounded professionals frequently seek or are sent to psychotherapy. At first, they may feel they have regressed or lost ground in their own maturation process. Feeling thrown backward, they reel from the blow and see therapy as a chance to return to where they were before the trauma. Therapy, to them, is a kind of crack-repair job, restoration rather than reconstruction. A new hopefulness about the future can emerge, but the hope may be based in fantasy.

Substance Abuse and the At-Risk

The condition of being at risk does not stop when sobriety begins. Substance abuse is widespread among professionals and accounts for a large portion of their medical expenses. In-patient treatment programs offer the substance abuser an opportunity to begin sobriety in a controlled and supportive setting away from the environment that stimulates and supports the abuse. Such treatment produces sobriety, which must be a precondition for therapy but is never a substitute for it. Nor are support groups the equivalent of therapy. I have never encountered a recovering person who did not also have significant underlying developmental damage. The use of expensive in-patient treatment as therapy or as cure for codependency is neither necessary nor effective. In almost all cases, psychotherapy is best done only after a recovering substance abuser has completed three months of sobriety and participated in ninety Alcoholics Anonymous meetings in ninety days.

The prognosis for recovery from substance abuse is guarded at best in spite of the simplicity and singlemindedness of the goals of treatment programs. The twelve-step model of Alcoholics Anonymous has proven the most effective of all models. Often an intervention involving friends and family and supported by a professional intervention expert is a powerful and effective beginning for treatment. However, those persons who would intervene in cases of substance abuse must truly care about those they hope to help. They must also understand that a recovered substance abuser remains a damaged person and that sobriety is only one step along the road to maturity. Whether intervening or receiving intervention, the professional should know its limitations.

For the religious professional private or public substance abuse can be a form of acting in or acting out, and when it interferes with professional functioning then it frequently precipitates a crisis. Among other behaviors that can become public and perpetuate crisis are sexual abuse, extramarital affairs, angry acting out, and immobilizing depression. Workaholism, extreme dependency, and damaging compulsiveness are usually less understood but can warn that help should be sought and psychotherapy begun. Occasionally upon psychological assessment, a candidate for a religious profession will show such pervasive developmental damage that intervention must be made and help sought before the candidacy can be supported.

Two Therapeutic Approaches

There are two alternative therapeutic approaches to the treatment of developmentally rooted damage; psychoanalytic and cognitive. Each begins from a different and seemingly contradictory central assumption, but each holds a similar understanding of successful outcome. Increasingly, however, mature therapists, regardless of their initial training, are becoming more eclectic. Most therapists use processes that can be identified with one school or the other.

Psychoanalytic psychotherapy has a long and successful history of defining, describing, and addressing developmentally rooted conditions. Analytic psychology has developed the large body of theory on which an understanding of these conditions is based. The theories of emotional development cited throughout this book are rooted in psychoanalytic psychology principally in the work of Kohut and Kernberg. Recently, cognitive psychological treatment has also developed approaches to long-term treatment of entrenched and distorting conditions (Beck and Freeman 1990). When utilized properly, the cognitive model, like the psychoanalytic, provides intensive, individual, long-term, and dynamic therapy. There are, however, many short-term treatment models being used today that are incapable of generating comprehensive change. Still other models may work with some developmentally rooted conditions and not with others. Therapies that are primarily behavior-oriented, family- or group-oriented, supportive, or twelve-step, for example, are appropriate for compulsive disorders, in part because compulsives tend to dissect more than reflect.

Psychoanalytic theory does not think in the categories of good or bad, but it does have its own categories: Neurotic or nonneurotic, developmentally damaged or not, sick or well, healthy or unhealthy, and reality-based or -distorted are but a few. Psychoanalytic theorists make judgments in large quantity but start from the conviction that it is important to resolve issues of early development in ways that ensure that they do not distort everyday life decisions and relationships.

The Best Time for Treatment

Middle adulthood is the best time for problem-resolving. Even cases that come to crisis and through it during young adulthood often require additional psychotherapeutic attention later. The later work will be easier, however, if early attention has been given.

Kernberg (1980, 121–53) indicates that middle adulthood is important for psychotherapy because experiences by then have accumulated. The adult is forced to take some responsibility for life and actions. Precipitants to action may take the form of failed relationships, career blows, or such family circumstances as the death of a parent or alienation from a child. The result is a kind of awakening and a renewal of the instinctual drive toward health described by Kohut (1984, 152–53) and Erikson (1959, 50–100).

There seems to be a sort of mid-life window that offers at-risk professionals an opportunity to live the second half of their adult lives in significantly more satisfying ways than they did the first half. It is quite exciting to contemplate this opportunity for middle-aged professional men and women. It may be the last major opportunity for reconstructive change and, if it is missed, the professional may spend the rest of his or her life defending against reality. Psychology serves to restructure the personality in order to free the person from his or her own wounds so that the individual can be more empathic and better able to make good decisions about relationships.

The Unresolved Issues

In understanding how things go wrong in the maturing process it is well to know what the process looks like under the best circumstances. There are developmental issues and developmental tasks that help move the child from the stage of narcissism to the beginnings of healthy separation-individuation (Kernberg 1980, 105–17). The relatively undamaged child makes this journey without interruption; the at-risk person does not. When severe damage has occurred, the therapist may later serve a parent's function in reparenting the damaged child who is now chronologically an adult.

Damage is often caused when a parent (traditionally the mother) has perceived the child as an extension of herself and cannot permit separation, or when a parent (traditionally the father) has not permitted *idealization* (a perception that he is better than good), thereby inhibiting the development of adequate *ego strength* (a separateness of self from others). In the first case the child becomes an adult who seeks constant gratification and adoration from others, being unable to provide it for him- or herself. In the latter, the resulting adult searches fruitlessly for the lost ideal. For clergy this lost ideal may be God.

Therapeutic Substitutes for Normal Development

Empathic Parenting.   An individual needs some experience with an accepting and self-confident adult. In therapy, the therapist must move from being seen by the patient as a distant, judging professional to being seen as the needed parent/lover, and then back again to being seen as a therapist who is totally other.

Maturation.   The substitute for maturation is seen in the resumption of an interrupted developmental process.

Internalization of a Mirroring Parent Figure (Self-esteem).   This is the internalization of a parent's approval in order to develop self-esteem. Once self-esteem is damaged by failure to internalize a parent's approval or love, it remains damaged. It is possible for damaged adults, however, to discover more self-love within themselves than they originally thought they had. Additional sources of self-esteem can be found in compensating external factors, such as status in profession or recognized achievement.

Internalization of an Idealized Parent Figure for Ego Strength.   Ego strength, once damaged, remains damaged. As the need for a perfect parent diminishes, the individual is free to make his or her own choices without reference to their compensation for lack of the ideal parent.

Resolution of Separation Issues.   When separation has not occurred, therapy can enable the patient to know the boundaries of the self and of others. The possibility exists of achieving a self separate enough to interact realistically with the environment.

Beginning Resolution of "Splitting" Issues.   Therapy can offer a patient the opportunity to begin to see things as whole and neither all bad nor all good, neither black nor white. This is something normally taught by parents and achieved in separation.

Beginning Ability to Postpone Pleasure.   The patient learns that the absence of pleasure is not pain or punishment. The infantile pleasure drive is modified by a better sense of reality.

THERAPY AND ASSESSMENT

The process of therapy often involves giving up that which we most believed we needed in order to survive. This is a difficult and threatening process. It needs to happen under secure circumstances and with a person who can be trusted and perceived as able to help. It does not, on the other hand, mean feeling comfortable. Trusting begins with believing that the therapist wants to work with the client. A good therapist has to show concern and credibility to his or her patient and establish a secure frame in which the treatment can happen. This frame is established in part by scheduling and keeping to a regular time, maintaining promptness for beginning and ending, and not changing or cancelling unless absolutely necessary. The therapist must also be firm about payment schedules. While these seem minor matters, they help to develop the trust that is essential in a quality therapeutic relationship.

For the at-risk professional who is used to fewer boundaries when working with members of the congregation, the therapeutic context is sometimes frustrating. Any good therapist knows what boundary-challenging processes to expect from each patient depending upon his or her defensive structure, and each patient reenacts characteristic defensive ploys. The therapeutic setting is a clearly defined stage, calculated to showcase definitive behavior of the patient on the way to insight, understanding, and maturing.

Choosing a Therapist

Choosing to work with a therapist is a major commitment. Is it best to select a therapist or to have one recommended by a trusted source? A problem for at-risk professionals in choosing a therapist is that the same dynamics are at play as in the selecting of marriage partners and lovers. When a future patient finds a therapist with whom they want to work, the choice may have been made from unconsciously driven distortions. It is even possible that the chosen therapist shares the same distortions and would unconsciously collude in maintaining the patient's pathology rather than encourage change.

It seems better to have a psychotherapist recommended by someone trusted. Authorities in religious organizations have usually had enough experience to be able to recommend psychotherapists to assist religious professionals. The degree of maturity they bring to their own professional ministries will determine the wisdom of those choices. If the authority is respected, then the choice is often accepted even if the desire to accept is part of the pathology. If the choice is forced or mandated, as it sometimes is, treatment becomes difficult. Some would say it becomes impossible.

Two other alternative procedures for choosing a therapist are possible. One may ask other trusted professionals, religious and otherwise, for three recommendations each. When recommendations coincide, the potential patient can interview the therapists and ask them about their experience, costs, and credentials. Make a choice following the interviews. A second alternative is to call therapists who are recommended and ask whom they would recommend if not themselves. The same names may begin to surface repeatedly. Both these methods have been frequently used with some success.

Almost no psychotherapist can hope to receive universal professional acclaim. The late, noted Lutheran theologian Joseph Sittler is reported to have asserted that he was a good enough theologian to know that he was not a great one. Good psychotherapists are much the same, good enough to know that they are not great and to know that therefore they cannot work with equal effectiveness on every prospective patient.

Is the gender of the therapist an issue? Some would argue that it is an important factor in successful therapeutic outcome. There is little or no data to support that notion. It may be important for initial patient comfort, but its importance is minimized over the entire period of therapy.

There is both a feminine and a masculine face to psychotherapy, and good psychotherapists have both. The feminine face is characterized by tenderness, nurturance, gentleness, and supportive consideration of others' needs, while the male face is characterized by aggressiveness, planning, seeing options, limit-setting, and boundary maintenance. A mature adult such as a good psychotherapist, easily, flexibly, and volitionally manifests both a feminine and a masculine face.

Is it necessary for the psychotherapist to have the same faith structure and theology as the patient? There are no significant studies to support the notion that the therapist's faith structure or lack of it has any bearing on effective treatment in intensive, individual, long-term therapy. Some research, however, has found negative impact on successful treatment when the therapist is a fundamentalist Christian.

A Strategy for the Future

Most ecclesiastical systems expect psychological assessments of candidates for religious professions. These assessments have varied widely in focus, content, and structure, and have met with mixed success in assuring religious systems of high-quality, mature professionals. Candidates, too, have had varied reactions to such assessments, ranging from anger or outrage to passive acceptance.

I believe that each candidate for a religious profession should undergo a dynamically oriented psychological assessment. There are at least three reasons for this.

First, systems can no longer assume a certain level of health or maturity of candidates for a religious profession. There was a time when religious systems operated from an assumption of health in screening candidates for a clerical profession. Several candidate assessment programs with which I am familiar continue to make this assumption. Current events in religious systems have made it clear that this assumption is fallacious: Data assembled over a period of thirty years suggest that candidates for religious professions are not as healthy as the general population. The damage that can be done by immature and dysfunctional religious professionals is too great to ignore.

Religious systems can now assume that most candidates have some level of dysfunction (the human condition), and that about one-third of the candidates have significant levels of dysfunction. Systems should begin by assuming that candidates have some dysfunction and then assess for degrees of dysfunction. Is the level of dysfunction presently or potentially debilitating or inhibiting? How can candidates be helped to address their unresolved material?

Second, religious systems need to be more willing to say no to unqualified candidates or candidates who are low-functioning and unresponsive to intervention. A dynamic assessment helps those in authority to confirm their own suspicions about certain candidates. Committee members need to be trained in dynamic assessment and interpretation, so that they can understand the language and conceptual frame of the diagnostician.

Third, intensive psychotherapy needs to be a normative part of the preparation process for religious professionals. No candidate expects to be harmful in his or her professional and personal functioning. Religious populations still resist the notion of intensive psychotherapy as a norm, although this resistance is slowly disappearing as increasing numbers of religious professionals get into difficulty. The climate for psychoanalytic psychotherapy is warming.

My own research suggests that approximately three-fourths of those clergy who appear most mature and have moved into positions of authority report that they have experienced major crisis or trauma and sought psychotherapeutic intervention. The sample I studied had been in full-time religious professional work for from fifteen to twenty-five years. The most mature professionals have weathered the crisis and found help in extended programs of therapy.

A second group of professionals active for the same length of time who have been judged as less mature and have usually moved only laterally in their profession report few major crises and little trauma. Only 15 percent of these ever sought psychotherapy. We can conclude that there is some connection between successful functioning and a history of crisis and therapeutic intervention. But prior to this study, the data have supported correlations between success and emotional health among other types of professionals. It is clear that religious professionals who are most effective in their work are ones who have taken their own dysfunction seriously and have moved on with their lives via psychotherapy (Weiser 1985).

The Dynamic Assessment

The most accurate predictions of the future are based on the evidence and meaning of the past. It is important to have a history of the distortions from the individual pasts that candidates bring with them into a religious profession. Past history and clinical data join present impressions as a basis for accurate judgment. Assessment takes the form of a clinical interview, dynamic test data, and other relevant data such as intelligence and general interests. This information can reveal developmental damage, pervasive characteristics, and unconscious material that cause distortions of perception.

Some popular tests such as the Meyers-Briggs Type Inventory (MBTI) would be ruled out by the dynamic assessment criterion. Although this instrument can be a useful tool for persons who want a quick, self-reported work and lifestyle profile, it is not a dynamic psychological test in the sense that individual unconsciously driven distortions pass unchanged into the results. All self-report instruments, including most of those used in organizational or marital consultations, have the same drawback. No measure of the distortion or the degree of distortion is built into the instrument. See the Appendix for a suggested comprehensive assessment.

A good clinician will not make observations unless they are supported by at least two sources of information. Those responsible for candidate decisions should be sure that they understand what the clinician is telling them and that they are speaking the same language. The decision makers and the clinician need to meet periodically for training in the conceptual frame of the diagnostician.

Dynamic assessments can be useful to religious systems as they look for the best way to encourage and support each candidate. They can be especially helpful in encouraging candidates to take the steps necessary to prevent or weather a crisis.

One word of caution: It is easy for the decision makers to put unjustified and excessive power in the hands of the assessor or the assessment. While this appeals to the narcissism of many clinicians, it is not in the long-term best interest of the religious system. If a candidate has issues that need to be dealt with in therapy or is not appropriate as a candidate, decision makers need to take full responsibility for this and not be tempted to blame the clinician or the tests if something goes wrong later. This is a further reason for the clinician and the decision makers to be clear about the goals of the assessment.

CONCLUSION: THE HEALTHY RELIGIOUS PROFESSIONAL

The task of a psychotherapist is a little like that of a midwife: It is to drag patients kicking and screaming into adulthood. The first several glimpses of adulthood are always terrifying. Most patients retreat in terror, eager to remain immature. But after many conversations, and against the forces of much resistance on their part, most patients finally accept maturity as the most viable of their options. They come to see it as preferable to the style they have been protecting so fiercely and defending so frequently.

THE PATH TO AWARENESS

Why does the acceptance of change take so long when patients coming into therapy insist so clearly that they want to get better? The fact is that most of a patient's energy is directed toward staying the same. Patients want to *feel* differently, not *be* different. They want to remain children and are unwilling to pay any personal price for change. They want the circumstances of their lives improved or other people improved, but not necessarily themselves. To change involves the painful process of growth, a process that is neither pleasant nor safe. So patients remain afraid to grow up. In each person hides a child who stopped growing up for fear that the journey to adulthood would result in death, insanity, or utter loneliness and isolation.

Freud called the energy directed toward *not* changing *resistance*. Another phrase, overused but useful, is the *child within* as popularized by Charles Whitfield (1987). That concept was used originally and most powerfully by Alice Miller in *The Drama of the Gifted Child* (1981).

If growing up is perceived as dangerous, and life as too hard to live, then what decision remains? The child determines to live as best he or

155

she can, not real life but a stilted and distorted variant of life. This ersatz life exists without awareness, and therefore without the fear of knowing. It is a life of partial emotions, empathic limitations, and damaged self.

What does this psychology propose as a way through the wounding and on to adulthood? Initially to regain intimacy with others and a sense of belonging, patients must dive deeply into themselves to recover the courage and the drive to mature that they possessed at the beginning.

Maturing is intended to be a single seamless process beginning at birth and extending through all of life. Identifiable life stages are helpful markers but are not separate incidents unrelated to the whole. A blocking, stopping, or inhibiting of the process creates one's problems. Patients must first look deep within to get the process back on track. When the wound is sufficiently healed, leaving its scar, a patient can come back, up, and out again into the world of others.

Drive and pursuit add spice to life. A knowledge of the probability of hurt can enhance life. Therefore some narcissism and some compulsivity are necessary. One needs to think well, sometimes overly well, of the self, and religious professionals also need to pay attention to the details of work and life, while knowing that "the devil lurks in the details." On the other hand, self-love and absorption in detail when found in extremes are signs of damage. Wounding is the norm; unaddressed wounds are the tragedy.

THE GROWING ACCEPTANCE OF PSYCHOLOGY

Some time in the recent past—it is difficult to pinpoint it exactly—the world as we knew it began to dissolve: The order of things understood, our cultural markers, our organizations, our neighborhood gathering places, the rituals, the belief systems, and the communities began to come apart. These were the things that held culture together and determined how life was supposed to unfold. They helped people know where they fit in and how things worked. Practically everyone accepted them.

Whether or not these preexisting systems were reasonable, just, or even humane, the point is that if one chose to stand outside them, it was clear what one was doing. There was a clear outside and a clear inside. Without the markers this clarity has disappeared, and not just a few people but nearly everyone feels like an outsider; hence the renewed interest in the process of belonging and the search for intimacy. Attention to relationships and awareness of differences are both heightened. Loneliness has indeed become the disease of the last several decades.

The Dutch Jesuit Henri Nouwen ([1972] 1979) said it well: "Maybe the word 'loneliness' best expresses our immediate experience. . . . We live in a society in which loneliness has become one of the most painful human wounds. The growing competition and rivalry which pervade our lives from birth have created in us an acute awareness of our isolation. This awareness has . . . left many with a heightened anxiety and the intense search for the experience of . . . community."

America has become a nation of strangers. Even more, we have become a planet of strangers who know about each other but do not know each other at all.

Things have not improved since Nouwen wrote his book. On the contrary, our decades of increasing wealth (and increasing poverty), the Me decade, the Greed decade, and whatever the present decade may label itself have not alleviated the problem. A simple solution will not emerge for a problem as endemic and pervasive as alienation. But alienation or loneliness are not the origins of wounding; they merely exaggerate the condition. Little wonder that maturity is for many a less than desirable goal. It is far too frightening to grow up in a place like this.

One attempt to alleviate alienation has been to make as much of the planet as possible uniform in appearance. It is as if safety lay in sameness. There has been profit in the enterprise, but not much satisfaction. Instead of a sense of security, our homogeneous highway systems and look-alike malls have produced a sort of George Orwell/Woody Allen nightmare. We have become a world of the bland, the dull, the trivial, and the mediocre.

In another attempt to counter the pervasive sense that something is wrong, we take one another's emotional temperature: "Are you happy?" "Are you fulfilled?" "Are you enriched?" "Is your relationship growing?" These questions would have been foreign and deeply embarrassing to my grandparents or even to many of our parents. It is as if we have finally, in the last thirty years, begun to explore the emotional side of life.

It is not surprising that psychotherapeutic applications of psychology have begun to find easy acceptance among larger numbers of professionals, despite the still-existing popular prejudice against psychotherapy. Remember that the discipline of psychology is little more than a century old, and in basic matters people change slowly. Psychology is just a more recent model for examining human woundedness and proposing a way to a more mature life.

Until World War II, the practice of psychology was limited to major urban areas such as New York, London, Berlin, Chicago, and Paris. Psychiatric work with military personnel in World War II expanded the parameters. Such best-sellers as Norman Vincent Peale's *The Power of Positive Thinking* (1952) and Dale Carnegie's *How to Win Friends and Influence People* ([1936] 1981) signaled the advent of pop psychology. These two books and the thousands that followed applied psychological concepts to human behavior in simplified ways. In less than fifty years, psychological concepts and jargon have become an integral part of both American and Western culture.

The psychological and philosophical formulations of woundedness have their theological counterparts. The Buddhist road, which moves from limited vision toward increased insight or understanding, and the Christian promise of exchanging bondage for freedom are but two examples.

With growing acceptance by professionals, psychological definitions and insights have recently been added to the already standard fare of the religious, the pseudo-religious, the philosophical, and the theological. Psychological explanations of the human condition compete with others, including religious ones, in the alternatives they would offer us. As recently as 1964 a church supervisor approved my participation in a sensitivity training session only with the proviso that I check back with him and with a psychiatrist upon my return. He wanted to make certain that I was still sane following the experience. Now, experientially based group education has become normative in many religious systems.

The sense that something is wrong, or the longing for something more or something different, connects contemporary culture with the primitive or primal, including the mythic and religious. Woundedness has been around for a long time; it is just that we had different ways to describe it. The Judaeo-Christian tradition, for example, refers to what is wrong with the human condition as sin and cites the myth of the Fall or alienation from God as its explanation. Many ancient mythologies from various cultures offer similar representations.

Within dynamic psychology, the common human condition is seen as the result of an interference in the childrearing process resulting in distortions and misperceptions.

MATURE LEADER, HEALTHY PROFESSIONAL

Congregations regularly create their own faith and theology to fit their own needs. Religious professionals work effectively with about 10 percent of the membership at any time, while the 90 percent are largely untouched. The mature professional knows the limits of ministry and can respond to the challenges of those limits. Mature congregational members respond from their own maturity, while the remaining members remain at their own defensive or immature levels.

It appears that more religious professionals are leaving than entering the profession. Newer professionals seem less open to change than candidates did a generation ago. One seminary faculty member indicated that the majority of students he sees have no desire for wisdom but view a seminary education as a necessary exercise and precondition to achieving their professional goals. Further, he says, they are not even open to reexamining their goals, which in many cases are the product of their own immaturity.

In some ways the history of Western religious systems is the history of ongoing conflict between the compulsives and the narcissists; mainline religious systems have found themselves either in periods of risk and active societal leadership, or in periods of system maintenance and caution. Thus the need is all the greater for mature professionals who fall into neither group. The immature goals of more recent candidates for religious professions will be unable to maintain the system in healthy, healing, and challenging ways. Such mature professionals might well become discouraged, knowing that they are influencing the lives of only 10 percent of the membership at any given time and that the remaining membership may be critical as well as beyond reach. The religious profession can be interpersonally dangerous and unsatisfying. But there are strong correlations between personal satisfaction and maturity, even when satisfaction must be found while the professional is interacting with immature people. This presupposes, however, that the mature religious professional does have some intimate and mature relationships.

Characteristics of a Healthy Professional

The characteristics of a healthy religious professional include a good orientation to reality, the ability to establish and maintain intimate longterm relationships, a sense of self in context, and a strong sense of separateness. Separateness is manifested by the professional's ability to know what material belongs to the *self* and what belongs to the *other*. The other is not permitted to spill into the self.

Healthy religious professionals maintain a more mature version of the pathological components with which they began. Of these defensive structures, the combination of narcissism and compulsivity in its mature forms with a depressed/dependent underpinning, contains the potential for the greatest professional success. Persons so characterized have sufficient separation and maintain safe distances from others. Their healthy narcissism prevents the very difficulty that its less mature form would have caused. Narcissism enables healthy distance and keeps the attention of others. The compulsive component enables mature people to listen carefully, pay attention to details, and plan well, but not by being obsessive about it. Histrionics in healthy form make for dramatic personal presentation, while healthy dependency makes for appropriate need for others.

Healthy professionals can flow easily between periods of disengaged reflection and intense engagement. They are able to be deliberate and spontaneous, their thought processes both free-flowing and intensely focused. The mature professional knows the limits of ministry and can respond realistically to the challenges of those limits. The professional needs a mild dose of depression in order to see the dark side of the reality of life. Some dependency for the healthy attachment and necessary leaning upon others complete the make-up of the healthy religious professional.

Balance and Integration

Healthy religious professionals recognize themselves to be ambivalent and at times contradictory collections of disparate components. They celebrate the pieces of themselves and they recognize integration, but as a conglomeration that is often out of balance, not as an ordered whole. They are not afraid to devote reflective attention to darker components when these pieces come to the surface. These clergy are as interested in themselves as they are in others. They do not analyze things to death but reflect on the whole of events. They can frame each encounter and experience with a beginning and an ending. They can withdraw or disengage before any significant encounter as a kind of preparatory experience. They know what it is like to sit in symbolic meditative circles waiting quietly for clarity and direction. They do not pursue answers frantically but are content to await the unfolding by actively and intently listening. Healthy professionals are familiar and comfortable with quiet and seek the desert, the mountain retreat, or the river shore. They are content with waiting and patient with the movement of events. With maturity, healthy professionals develop their tolerance for and pleasure in the ambivalent nature of almost everything.

Margaret Rioch (1970) describes the delicate balance that exists between leader and member at all times. The leader is simultaneously sheep and shepherd. A leader is therefore always at risk of being symbolically killed by the membership as simultaneous guide and sacrifice.

MATURITY FOR ADULTS

The mature adult can experience the full range of emotion from rage to ecstasy without the neurotic need for extremes or constriction. Extreme feelings do not disappear; rather, they take their place within a rich emotional spectrum that also includes boredom, now seen as calm. Real life elicits real emotion that is appropriate to the experience. Less prominent in the mature emotional range are childish emotions such as confusion and upset.

There is a persistent notion that dampening of the neurotic fire correlates with the loss of creativity. This is rooted in a false connection between creativity, eccentricity, and pathology, one often found in the myth of the crazy artist in literature and art. There is some correlation, though apparently not a strong one, between manic-depression and creative output. Being mature does not mean being dull or uninteresting— indeed, the contrary is true. Maturing persons have more energy for the intense and creative parts of their lives because they are not expending energy in the defense of the self. Mature persons no longer need to be the center of a personal universe but are able to live as one entity among many others floating and interacting in a chaotic universe.

The characteristics of the maturing person include the following abilities:

1. to love and to work
2. to tolerate ambivalence
3. no longer to be filled with self
4. to see life in paradoxical tension

Mature people have good impulse control and good reality orientation. They establish and maintain healthy relationships, defined here as separated, as opposed to undifferentiated or codependent. Mature people are very much alive in the present, which gives them free access to and from liminal states.

Mature people have empathy and can love. They are whole people whose earlier splitting has been healed. The passion of the darker side and the clarity of the intellect are theirs and are integrated within them. Mature people are still wounded and they know it, but they have accepted life as a process rather than as a goal to be achieved. There are still unknown parts of the self within mature people, and some of these may well never be known.

Freud defined normality in surprisingly simple terms: to love and to work *(lieben und arbeiten)*. By the term *love* he meant expansive generosity as well as sexual or genital love. When he said *love and work,* he meant productiveness that would not preoccupy an individual so much that his or her capacity to be a sexual and loving being would be lost (Erikson 1959).

Balance: An Elusive Goal

A common systems notion is that the whole is different from (not necessarily greater than) the parts. But the Torah teaches the same. The whole is not even the sum of its parts, as is claimed in elementary mathematics. The whole is the whole, consisting of huge amounts of something and of nothing all at the same time, balanced and unbalanced at the same time, sensible and chaotic at the same time, incredibly beautiful and simultaneously paradoxical, relaxed, and filled with tension.

Since the time of the Greeks, who decided that all wholes consisted of identifiable parts such as body, mind, and spirit, we have believed that everything is divisible into components. The way to get it all is to get all the parts. Semitic cultures are more fortunate in some ways; they have never fallen prey to this Greek concept and continue in both language and conceptual frame to view a whole simply as a whole.

Equal parts do not always make up a whole. People want too many things and in too great a quantity. They want enormous helpings of success, love, good relationships, money, sex, power, prestige, accomplishment, experience, as well as unlimited virtue and the benefit of the seven deadly sins with none of the consequences. It does not take long to discover that we are not going to get all those things.

Nevertheless, most people view their lives as consisting of parts. Furthermore, they see clear phases of their lives as components. Not too many years ago, stage theory based on the work of Erik Erikson (1959) divided the whole of life into pieces or stages. The theory presupposed clearly identifiable phases and a predictable course to be followed by all. Influenced by Daniel Levinson's, *Seasons of a Man's Life* (1978) and Gail Sheehy's popular *Passages* (1974, 1976), people believed that the life course was divided into inevitable chapters in a process that began at birth and concluded with death. The life-stage revolution identified stages for everything from divorce to job change. This theoretical frame began to crumble shortly after its inception when people discovered its inconsistency of application. Men and women, for example, were seen to experience chronological stages differently and to different ends. Even more tellingly, neither all men nor all women followed the same progression of stages.

One study (Farrell and Rosenberg 1981, 80) established that only 12 percent of all males experienced anything akin to a traumatic transition into middle adulthood. Carol Gilligan (1982) demonstrated that women's experiences and values are different from those of men. Anne Wilson Schaef and Diane Fassel (1988) argued that such a determinatively male phenomenon as the "old boy network" now has many "old girls" in it and is becoming multiracial.

Indeed, sisterhood seems to be growing, but it has a long way to go. While the old boy network lacks emotional depth and is devoid of intimacy, it is clearly present and powerful. Sisterhood seems more clusterlike and apparently does not yet exist on a grand scale even approaching the old boy version.

Most people take the "parts" of themselves from some accepted list either of static attributes or of life stages, and they pursue each one, believing that life will be fulfilling if all are achieved. Success, love, intimacy, and spiritual well-being, to name a few, are pursued as if they are separate entities. Yet many people complete the life list and still sense that something is wrong, because the pieces do not equal a whole and the whole itself lacks balance and realism.

Balance is an elusive goal to pursue. No one has scoops of seven different life flavors in some sort of equal bowl; most of us have a lot of one flavor and perhaps none of another. Some who have a lot of one flavor look into their neighbor's bowl and think that what they have is wrong, because the neighbor has something different. We reduce our notion of the possible and thus mourn the absence of the missing pieces. We miss the celebrating of our gifts and blessings.

Sesame Place

Sesame Place is a park for preschool children in Bucks County, Pennsylvania. One of the experiences it offers is a large cage filled with balls of different colors. The children jump into the mass of balls and play. They cannot sink, but they can burrow and be completely covered, or they can crawl around on the top. It looks like great fun, but adults are not permitted to enter the cage.

What if we added one more ball? What if the ball were the brightest of bright red? What if after we played in the cage we went to get a hot dog? What if we talked for a while and then came back to the cage? What has happened to the brightest of the bright red balls? It is there—somewhere.

Reality! Reality is my brightness mixed with all the others. Children often find the bright red ball before adults do, for the same reason that children know the right questions to ask and do not hesitate to ask them. How is the world? How does it work? What is real? Pinocchio knew. He knew that the kind of reality we know was not within the realm of his experience, but he wanted desperately to be real. Pinocchio came to know the reality that Geppetto showed him:

- that the world is filled with possibilities and terror simultaneously
- that we can get some of the things we want, but not all of them
- that we are not the center of the universe, and there is nothing we can do about it
- that it is usually all right not to be the center
- that injustice, unfairness, and inequality exist
- that change—things becoming different than they are—is one of life's few certainties
- that people die, people get sick, and accidents happen for no reason
- that some people love you for right and wrong reasons
- that some people dislike you and even hate you, for right and wrong reasons
- that you are not the strongest, the most beautiful, or even the brightest, but that this is all right too
- that people and systems will disappoint, but they can also support and please you
- that expecting too much from too few always means failure
- that you can choose to love someone and be committed to them in ways that are not destructive
- that there is almost always more than one option
- that there is almost always more than one way to look at things
- that the circumstances of life cannot be predicted and often have no purpose
- that if meaning, understanding, or wisdom is gained from experience, it is always after the fact
- that everything that happens is part of the total experience
- that almost everything requires some confidence in yourself, but neither boastfulness nor a demeaning attitude is helpful
- that stories do not all end the same way.

THE ROAD AHEAD

We are always in the process of endings, transitions, and new beginnings. Parts of ourselves remain unfinished, childish, and infantile. Damage or wounding is a permanent state of affairs—no cosmetic surgery will make the wound go away. At best the goal is to keep the past in the past and not in the present.

When one no longer needs to protect oneself or maintain distortions, there is a great release of time and energy. The individual is driven out of the self, no longer needing to be filled with self alone. Energy now exists for going out of the self to others. This is the empathy of the healed wounded.

The mature person discovers empathically that the world is filled with others. These others cannot but be visible once self-absorption has diminished. Rigidity, too, disappears, and with it the need for easy answers to complex problems.

The drive to belong or to be separate can be neurotic. By nature, one simultaneously belongs and is separate. In the mature person, the neurotic drive is replaced by a sense of belonging to a complex, paradoxical, tension-filled, unfair, unjust, loving, supportive, and often surprising human family. This family is comprised mainly of other wounded people who, as all wounded do, react out of more primitive emotional selves.

The neurotic drive to belong can be replaced by the satisfaction of that drive—in other words, by belonging. When one belongs, one is willing to pay the cost of that belonging. The cost includes compromise, sacrifice, and patience. One possible conclusion is that maturity drives one both to recognize belonging and to desire it. We recognize that the drive to belong is as basic as the need to be loved or the drive to satisfy hunger. Individualism, particularly its singularly unthinking and unreflective American variant, has run its course.

In recent years, the literature of personal growth and the literature of social responsibility have seemed mutually exclusive. This book concludes with the concept that a healing of the wound is the first requirement for authentic belonging. Personal maturity and social responsibility are responses to the same two-part question: First, what are human beings? And second, what is the nature of their interrelationships? The processes that correspond to these questions drive deeply into the self and out again. They are integrally related.

APPENDIX

A comprehensive dynamic assessment might include the following instruments. The battery was prepared by the author and Jack Lit, Ph.D., ABPP, an associate of the author in Systems Therapy and Consultation Services, Allentown, Pennsylvania.

1. A Comprehensive Clinical Interview

This process pays particular attention to developmental themes, personal dynamics, and the dynamics of the family of origin. It is a history-taking process.

2. Tests of Personality Structure

Rorschach. This projective test is particularly helpful in determining primary style themes and revealing unconscious material that fuels distortion.

Minnesota Multiphasic Personality Inventory (MMPI and MMPI-2). The MMPI is the grandparent of statistically constructed paper-and-pencil personality tests, and its revised version continues to be useful in identifying underlying themes and pervasive characteristics of personality. It is the single most used psychological test in the world. Although originally constructed for use with hospitalized patients, this is widely and effectively used with more normal populations. The revised version is used with increasing frequency because it is more sensitive to inclusive language and eliminates some of the harsher questions. The reliability of the original remains superior, although this may change as use of the revised version spreads and additional research is conducted.

Millon Clinical Multiaxial Inventory (MCMI). This is a relatively new instrument, designed for use with persons in psychotherapy. It is constructed around the assumption that the test taker is aware of problems and is seeking assistance. The diagnostic categories are more consistent with DSM III-R. Some consider the MCMI to be an alternative to the MMPI or MMPI-2.

The Sentence Completion Test, Thematic Apperception Test (TAT), or *Projective Drawings Test* may also provide useful clues to underlying personality structures.

3. Test of Intelligence and Cognitive Function

Wechsler Adult Intelligence Scale—Revised (WAIS-R). For the purposes of candidate assessment for a religious profession, it is useful to administer several of the subtests that correlate highly with overall intelligence. These include vocabulary, information, and similarities. The use of the digit span or digit symbol subtest scan may be a quick scan for learning disability. If such is suspected, a Bender-Gestalt or an Aphasia Screening Test may be a useful adjunct to the test battery. The use of the WAIS-R can be enhanced almost like a projective in that much useful information can be induced from the ways in which candidates answer questions.

Religious systems need not be overly concerned with the intelligence of their candidates. Even though the level of intelligence remains sufficiently high, it has lowered over the last twenty years. This test will help the assessor know something about thinking styles and general intelligence, which will offer predictions about success with theological education. The data can be coupled with academic success data from transcripts and interview.

4. Interest Tests

Strong Campbell Interest Inventory (SCII). John Holland, the godfather of career assessment, is reported to have said that giving someone an interest profile is about the same as sitting down with them and asking them what they are interested in. Nevertheless, this interest inventory can provide clues to a candidate's approach to academic material, and it is also a possible screen for depression or other characterological material.

BIBLIOGRAPHY

Amore, F. and A. Gennaro. 1985. Evoluzione del concetto di ambivalenza nella teoria freudiana: Prima Parte (Evolution of the ambivalence concept in Freudian psychology: Part 1). *Giornale Storico di Psicologia Dinamica* 9, 18 (June): 135–54. Describes the evolution of the concept of ambivalence.

Appignanesi, R. 1979. *Freud for beginners.* New York: Pantheon Books.

Baker, H. S. 1979. The conquering hero quits: Narcissistic factors in underachievement and failure. *American Journal of Psychotherapy* 33, 3: 418–27.

Bainton, R. H. 1956. *The age of the reformation.* Princeton: D. Van Nostrand Inc.

Banks, S., W. T. Mooney, R. J. Mucowski, and R. Williams. 1984. Progress in the evaluation and prediction of successful candidates for religious careers. *Counseling and Values* 28, 2: 82–91.

Beck, A., and A. Freeman. 1990. *Cognitive therapy of personality disorders.* New York: Guilford Press.

Benjamin, H. 1966. *The transsexual phenomenon.* New York: Julia Press Inc.

Bettelheim, B. 1982. *Freud and man's soul.* New York: Vintage Books.

Bion, W. R. 1984. *Second thoughts: Selected papers on psycho-analysis.* New York: Jason Aronson.

Bloom, J. H. 1971. Who become clergy? *Journal of Religion and Health* 10: 50–76.

Bowen, M. 1978. *Family therapy in clinical practice.* New York: Jason Aronson.

169

Brown, L. M., and Gilligan, C. 1992. *Meeting at the crossroads: Women's psychology and girls' development*. Massachusetts: Harvard University Press.

Bulfinch, T. 1955. *Mythology: The age of fable*. New York: Random House.

Bursten, B. 1982. Narcissistic personalities in DSM III: Personality classification. *Comprehensive Psychiatry* 23, 5: 409–20.

Cardwell, S. 1982. Why women fail/succeed in ministry: Psychological factors. *Pastoral Psychology* 30, 4 (Summer): 153–62. The study found that success was attributable to greater intelligence, sensitivity to feelings, greater leadership skills, tolerance of opposing viewpoints, and assertiveness in their own lives.

Carnegie, D. 1936, rev. ed. 1981. *How to win friends and influence people*. New York: Simon and Schuster.

Celmer, V., and J. Winer. 1990 Female aspirants to the Roman Catholic priesthood. *Journal of Counseling and Development* 69, 2 (November–December): 178–83. Finds a greater incidence of job dissatisfaction among women than among parish priests and nonparish priests, but found greater psychological dysfunction among both groups of priests than among the women.

Clancier, A. 1991. Novelty, trauma and writing. *Revue Française de Psychanalyse* 55, 1 (January–February): 203–7. Discusses the appearance of narcissistic qualities in writers, artists, physicians, psychoanalysts, and psychiatrists.

Clements, C. D. 1982. Misusing psychiatric models: The culture of narcissism. *Psychoanalytic Review* 69, 2: 283–95.

Colman, A. D., and W. H. Bexton, eds. 1975. *Group relations reader*. Sausalito, Calif.: GREX.

Cooper, A. M. 1984. Narcissism in normal development. In *Character pathology: Theory and treatment*. New York: Brunner-Mazel.

Corman, L. 1975. The dynamic understanding of narcissism. *Evolutionary Psychiatry* 40, 4: 729–57.

Cureton, C. B. 1983. Missionary fit: A criterion-related model. *Journal of Psychology and Theology* 11, 3: 196–202.

Daniel, S., and M. Rogers. 1981. Burn-out and the pastorate: A critical review with implications for pastors. *Journal of Psychology and Theology* 9, 3 (Fall): 232–49. Symptoms of burnout, such as increased defensiveness, fatigue, and exhaustion, are discussed as they relate to problems associated with clergy members.

Davis, J. A. 1982. Achievement variables and class cultures: Family, schooling, jobs, and forty-nine dependent variables in the cumulative GSS. *American Sociological Review* 47, 5: 569–86.

de Laender, J. 1978. The concept of narcissism and Freud's misrepresentation of his theory of instincts. *Psychologica Belgica* 18, 1:1–11.

Dervin, D. 1982. Steve and Adam and Ted and Dr. Lasch: The new culture and the culture of narcissism. *Journal of Psychohistory* 9, 3: 354–73.

Diagnostic and statistical manual of mental disorders, 3rd ed. 1980. Washington, D.C.: American Psychiatric Association.

Diagnostic and statistical manual of mental disorders, 3rd ed., rev. 1987. Washington, D.C.: American Psychiatric Association.

Doohan, H. 1982. Burn out: A critical issue for the 1980s. *Journal of Religion and Health* 21, 4 (Winter): 352–58. Attributes burn-out to increased demands on clergy members, and suggests that increased leisure may prevent the onset of burn-out.

Douglas, W. G. 1957. *Predicting ministerial effectiveness.* Ph.D. diss., Harvard University.

Drake, R. E., F. C. Osher, et al. 1991. Homelessness and dual diagnosis. *American Psychologist* 46, 11.

Duruz, N. 1981. Introductory notes to the study of narcissism. *Evolutionary Psychiatry* 47, 1: 3–22.

Eigen, M. 1985. The sword of grace: Flannery O'Connor, Wilfred R. Bion, and D. W. Winnicott. *Psychoanalytic Review* 72, 2 (Summer): 335–46. Asserts that the expansion undergone by psychoanalytic theory in the past several decades permits its application to literature and religion in ways that can no longer be described as reductionistic.

Eissler, K. R. 1975. The fall of man. *Psychoanalytic Study of the Child* 30: 589–646.

Encyclopedia of social work. 1987. Prevalence of mental illness. Washington, D.C.: National Assoc. of Social Workers.

Erikson, E. H. 1959. *Identity and the life cycle.* New York: International University Press Inc.

Falbo, T., L. New, and M. Gaines, 1987. Perceptions of authority and the power strategies used by clergymen. *Journal for the Scientific Study of Religion* 26, 4: 499–507. Finds little support for the assumption that clergy prefer to use those strategies consistent with their basis of authority.

Farrell, M. P., and S. D. Rosenberg. 1981. *Men at midlife.* Dover, Mass.: Auburn House Publishing Co.

Fausel, D. F. 1988. Helping the healer heal: Co-dependency in helping professionals. *Journal of Independent Social Work* 3, 2: 35–45. Argues that social workers who have their own problems with alcohol or other substances may be ineffective or harmful to chemically dependent clients.

Fine, R. 1986. The forgotten man: Understanding the male psyche. *Current Issues in Psychoanalytic Practice* 3, 2–4 (Summer–Winter): 1–368. Examines the male psyche in terms of sexuality, aggression, and the social role. Topics include power, success, narcissism, the average man, and therapists and clergy.

Freud, S. 1921. Group psychology and the analysis of the ego. Trans. and ed. J. Strachey. 1959. New York: W. W. Norton and Company.

———. 1927. *The future of an illusion.* Trans. J. Strachey. 1961. New York: W. W. Norton and Company.

Freyberg, J. T. 1984. The psychoanalytic treatment of narcissism. *Psychoanalytic Psychology* 1, 2: 99–112.

Friedman, E. H. 1985. *Generation to generation: Family process in church and synagogue.* New York: Guilford Press.

Gardner, H. 1978. *Developmental psychology: An introduction.* Boston: Little, Brown and Company.

Gay, P. 1982. Liberalism and regression. *Psychoanalytic Study of the Child* 37: 523–45. Defines liberalism as a capacity for tolerating the delays, disappointments, and ambiguities attendant upon any open society.

Gay, V. P. 1983. Ritual and self-esteem in Victor Turner and Heinz Kohut. *Zyton Journal of Religion and Science* 18, 3 (September): 271–81. Presents a paper given at a symposium on ritual in human adaptation.

Gediman, H. K. 1975. Reflections on romanticism, narcissism, and creativity. *Journal of the American Psychoanalytic Association* 23, 2: 407–23.

Gilligan, C. 1982. *In a different voice: psychological theory and women's development.* Massachusetts: Harvard University Press.

Goffman, E. 1963. *Stigma.* Englewood, N.J.: Prentice-Hall.

Golden, Charles J. 1979. *Clinical interpretation of objective psychological tests*. New York: Grune and Stratton.

Gordon, R. M. Interview with author, 19 October 1984.

Graham, J. R. 1977. *The MMPI: A practical guide*. New York: Oxford University Press.

Growth in ministry. 1976. Division for Professional Leadership, Lutheran Church in America in company with American Lutheran Church and Association of Evangelical Lutheran Churches. Philadelphia. The original research data of this project remains unpublished and is in the archives of the Evangelical Lutheran Church in America, Chicago.

Haley, J. 1971. *Changing families: A family therapy reader*. New York: Grune and Stratton.

Hamilton, L. H. 1989. In pursuit of the ideal: Narcissism and the performing artist. Ph.D. diss., Adelphi University, Garden City, N.Y.

Harder, D. W. 1979. The assessment of ambitious-narcissistic character style with three projective tests: The early memories, TAT, and Rorschach. *Journal of Personality Assessment* 43, 1: 23–32.

Harrington, P. 1984. Mary and femininity: A psychological critique. *Journal of Religion and Health* 23, 3 (Fall): 204–17. Suggests that the Virgin Mary in modern Catholicism relates to Freud's idea of "normal femininity," and places the Christian in the role of the child, receiving gratification from the mother.

Hoffer, E. 1951. *The true believer*. New York: Harper & Row.

Horney, K. 1939. *New ways in psychoanalysis*. New York: W. W. Norton and Company.

Humphries, R. H. 1982. Therapeutic neutrality reconsidered. *Journal of Religion and Health* 21, 2 (Summer): 124–31. Suggests that therapists' tendency to ignore the impact of their own religious beliefs on their patients constitutes an area of potential abuse of psychotherapy.

Hyman, R. B., and P. Woog. 1989. Flexibility, the dominant characteristic of effective helpers: A factor analytic study. *Measurement and Evaluation in Counseling and Development* 22, 3 (October): 151–57.

Jacques, E. 1970. *Work, creativity and social justice*. New York: International Universities Press.

Johnson, R. A. 1973. *Congregations as nurturing communities: A study of nine congregations of the Lutheran Church in America*. Philadelphia: Division for Parish Services.

Kadel, T. E., ed. 1980. *Growth in ministry*. Division for Professional Leadership, Lutheran Church in America in company with American Lutheran Church and Association of Evangelical Lutheran Churches. Philadelphia: Fortress Press.

Kalliopuska, M. 1991. Empathy, self-esteem and other personality factors among junior ballet dancers. *British Journal of Projective Psychology* 36, 2: 47–61.

Keddy, P., P. Erdberg, and S. Sammon. 1990. The psychological assessment of Catholic clergy and religious referred for residential treatment. *Pastoral Psychology* 38, 3 (Spring): 147–50. Examines the frequency of psychological disturbances among male and female clergy and religious, and finds the clergy more likely to develop naïve defensiveness, intellectualized orientation, and problems handling emotions. Males were found to have difficulty with their sexual orientation.

Kernberg, O. F. 1968. Factors in the psychoanalytic treatment of narcissistic personalities. *Psychotherapy Research Project of the Menninger Foundation*. Boston.

———. 1975. *Borderline conditions and pathological narcissism*. New York: Jason Aronson.

———. 1980. *Internal world and external reality: Object relations theory applied*. New York: Jason Aronson.

———. 1984. *Object relations theory and clinical psychoanalysis*. New York: Jason Aronson.

———. 1989. An ego psychology object relations theory of the structure and treatment of pathologic narcissism: An overview. *Psychiatric Clinics of North America* 12, 3 (September): 723–29. Summarizes the psychoanalytic understanding of narcissistic personality disorders and psychotherapeutic techniques for treatment of these patients.

———. 1990. Countertransference. *Classics in Psychoanalytic Technique*. Northvale, N.J.: Jason Aronson.

Kiley, D. 1983. *The Peter Pan syndrome*. New York: Avon.

Kinston, W. 1982. An intrapsychic developmental schema for narcissistic disturbance. *International Review of Psychoanalysis* 9, 3: 253–61.

Kleiger, J. 1990. Emerging from the 'dark night of the soul': Healing the false self in a narcissistically vulnerable minister. *Psychoanalytic Psychology* 7, 2 (Spring): 211–24. Examines the concept of conditional mirroring and its prevalence in certain clergy. This false-self experience may contribute to a sense of disillusionment and despair.

Klein, M. 1963. *Our adult world*. New York: Basic Books.

Kohut, H. 1971. *The analysis of the self: A systemic approach to the psychoanalytic treatment of narcissistic personality disorders*. New York: International Universities Press, Inc.

———. 1977. *The restoration of the self*. New York: International Universities Press, Inc.

———. 1984. *How does analysis cure?* Chicago: University of Chicago Press.

Kopp, S. B. 1972. *If you meet the Buddha on the road, kill him!* Ben Lomond, California: Science and Behavior Books.

Kovel, J. 1990. Beyond the future of an illusion: Further reflections on Freud and religion. *Psychoanalytic Review* 77, 1 (Spring): 69–87. Discusses Freud's preoccupation with religion, a subject he held in contempt as a universal neurosis and impediment to human growth.

Krakowski, A. 1984. Stress and the practice of medicine. III. Physicians compared with lawyers. *Psychotherapy and Psychosomatics* 42, 1–4 (November): 143–51. Compares the effects of stress on lawyers as opposed to physicians. Physicians demonstrated greater compulsivity, compulsive personality disorder, less tolerance for frustration, and more depression.

Kung, H. 1979. *Freud and the problem of God*. Trans. E. Quinn. New Haven: Yale University Press. Original lectures given in 1978.

Lachar, D. 1974. *The MMPI: Clinical assessment and automated interpretation*. Los Angeles: Western Psychological Services.

Lacocque, P. E. 1984. Fear of engulfment and the problem of identity. *Journal of Religion and Health* 23, 3 (Fall): 218–28. Death anxiety as linked to introspection and the search for identity. Gives an overview of hero myths and legends with engulfment motifs and presents a critical appraisal of Carl Jung's interpretation of its symbolism and relationship to "heroism" (that is, mental health).

Larousse encyclopedia of mythology. 1959. New York: Prometheus Press.

Larson, D., et al. 1988. The couch and the cloth: The need for linkage. *Hospital and Community Psychiatry* 39, 10 (October): 1064–68. Data from the Epidemiologic Catchment Area study were used to compare the demographic characteristics and psychiatric symptoms of persons classified into four groups based on source of mental health services: clergy only, mental health specialists only, both clergy and mental health specialists, and neither source. The data made clear the need for formal linkages between clergy and mental health professionals.

Lasch, C. 1978. *The culture of narcissism: American life in an age of diminishing expectations*. New York: W. W. Norton and Company.

LeCroy, C. 1986. Factors associated with burnout in the social services: An exploratory study. *Journal of Social Service Research* 10, 1 (Fall): 23–39. Suggests that burnout is closely associated with job situation, although personality factors such as self-esteem and autonomy play a crucial role in worker effectiveness.

Lederer, W. J., and D. D. Jackson. 1968. *The mirages of marriage*. New York: W. W. Norton and Company.

Lerner, H. 1984. Patterns of object relations in neurotic, borderline and schizophrenic patients. *Psychiatry* 4, 1 (February): 77–92. Analyzes the Rorschach protocols of, among others, fifteen borderline inpatients. Tests revealed the borderlines functioned at the highest developmental level of differentiation and articulation. The borderline diagnosis, according to the study, should be conceptualized along a continuum of severity.

Levinson, D. J. 1978. *The seasons of a man's life*. New York: W. W. Norton and Company.

Lewis, C. S. 1980. *The weight of glory*. New York: MacMillan.

Lindbeck, G. 1981. Lutheran churches. In *Ministry in America: A report and analysis, based on an in-depth survey of 47 denominations in the United States and Canada, with interpretation by 18 experts*, ed. D. S. Schuller, M. P. Strommen, and M. L. Brekke, 414–44. San Francisco: Harper and Row.

Loewenstein, S. 1977. An overview of the concept of narcissism. *Social Casework* 58, 3: 136–42.

Lovett, I. 1980. Pastor on a pedestal. In *Growth in ministry*, ed. T. E. Kadel, 81–93. Philadelphia: Fortress Press.

Macaskill, N. D. 1988. Personal therapy in the training of the psychotherapist: Is it effective? *British Journal of Psychotherapy* 4, 3 (Spring): 219–26.

Maeder, T. 1989. Wounded healers. *The Atlantic* (January): 37–47. The "helping professions," notably psychotherapy and the ministry, appear to attract more than their share of the emotionally unstable.

Marshall, J. 1986. Towards ecological understanding of occupational stress. *International Review of Applied Psychology* 35, 3 (July): 271–

86. Understanding levels of stress associated with a certain occupation depends upon the definition and stereotypes of the role occupied.

May, R. 1967. *The Art of Counseling*. New York: Abingdon Press.

———. 1975. *The Courage to Create*. New York: W. W. Norton and Company.

Mazlish, B. 1982. American narcissism. *Psychohistory Review* 10, 3–4: 185–202.

Medlicott, R. W. 1971. The sickness of Hercules. Some omnipotence of the narcissistic personality. *Australian and New Zealand Journal of Psychiatry* 11, 4: 213–17.

Mehl, L. G. 1979. Nurturing and mythus bearing in clergy work motivation. *Journal of Religion and Health* 18, 1: 29–37.

———. Interview with author, 13 October 1985.

———. The quality of ministerial candidates from a counselor's perspective. Paper presented to Lancaster Career Development Center Board, Lancaster, Pa., March 1991.

———. Interview with author, 18 November 1992.

Meloy, J. 1986. Narcissistic psychopathology and the clergy. *Pastoral Psychology* 35, 1 (Fall): 50–55. Suggests there is a higher incidence of psychopathology among clergy members because of the nature of the occupation; there is reinforcement for the personality problems such as a sense of entitlement, fear of dependency, detachment, or rage.

Miller, A. 1981. *The drama of the gifted child*. Trans. Ruth Ward. New York: Basic Books.

Miller, R. 1991. Saul Bellow: A biography of the imagination. *The New Republic* 204, 3 (April 1): 43.

Millon, T. 1977. *Millon Clinical Multiaxial Inventory*, 3d ed. Minneapolis: Interpretive Scoring Systems.

———. 1981. *Disorders of personality: DSM III, Axis II*. New York: John Wiley and Sons.

Minuchin, S. 1974. *Families and family therapy*. Massachusetts: Harvard University Press.

Nauss, A. 1972. Measuring ministerial effectiveness. *Journal of the Scientific Study of Religion* 11: 141–51.

———. 1973. The ministerial personality: Myth or reality? *Journal of Religion and Health* 12: 77–96.

Nouwen, H. J. M. 1979. *The wounded healer: Ministry in contemporary society*. Garden City, N. Y.: Image Books.

Oliner, M. M. 1978. Narcissism: Theoretical formulations of Bela Grunberger. *Psychoanalytic Review* 65, 2: 239–52.

Ogdon, Donald P. 1977. *Psychodiagnostics and personality assessment: A handbook*, 2d ed. Los Angeles: Western Psychological Services.

Ornstein, P. H., ed. *The search for the self: Selected writings of Heinz Kohut: 1950–1978*. Vol. 1. New York: International Universities Press, Inc.

Pauker, J. D. 1961. Psychological consultation and the referral. *Archives of General Psychiatry* 4 (February): 192–98. Discusses what may reasonably be expected of the clinical psychologist when he or she is asked for a psychological evaluation of a patient. Several points are emphasized: the kinds of questions that may most profitably be put to the clinical psychologist, the content of the referral, the kind of referral data that results in the most valid, useful, economical, and rapid evaluation, and the professional ethics and responsibilities of the clinical psychologist in the psychodiagnostic role. Much of the discussion centers about the intellectual and personality evaluations and the content of the psychological report.

Patrick, J. 1990. Assessment of narcissistic psychopathology in the clergy. *Pastoral Psychology* 38, 3 (Spring): 173–80. Finds that male clergy were not more narcissistic than the general population, although they were found to be more dominant. Female clergy were found to have a greater vulnerability for narcissism.

Peale, N. V. 1952. *The power of positive thinking*. New York: Prentice-Hall.

Prevalence of serious mental illness. 1990. *American Journal of Psychiatry*. Washington, D.C.: American Psychiatric Assoc. (December).

Prifetira, A., and J. J. Ryan. 1984. Validity of the Narcissistic Personality Inventory (NPI) in a psychiatric sample. *Journal of Clinical Psychology* 40, 1: 140–42.

Quadrio, C. 1982. The Peter Pan and Wendy syndrome: A marital dynamic. *Australian and New Zealand Journal of Psychiatry* 16, 2: 23–28.

Randolf, E. M., and C. A. Dye. 1981. The Peter Pan profile: Development of a scale to measure reluctance to grow up. *Adolescence* 16, 64.

Raskin, R. N. 1980. Narcissism and creativity: Are they related? *Psychological Reports* 46, 1: 55–60.

Rayburn, C., L. Richmond, and L. Rogers. 1986. Men, women, and religion: Stress within leadership roles. *Journal of Clinical Psychology* 42, 3 (May): 540–46. Studies various religious leaders in terms of occupational and personal stress experienced. Religious leaders exhibited less stress and demonstrated more personal resources compared to the general population. Ministers showed the highest amount of stress of all religious professionals.

Redl, F. 1980. Group emotion and leadership. In *Psychoanalytic Group Dynamics*, ed. S. Scheidlinger. New York: International Universities Press, Inc.

Reich, W. 1949. *Character analysis*. New York: Orgone Institute Press.

Reigstad, S. 1980. The development of the concept of narcissism in psychoanalytic thinking. *Norwegian Psychoanalytic Journal* 17, 6: 286–91.

Richmond, L., C. Rayburn, and L. Rogers. 1985. Clergymen, clergywomen, and their spouses: Stress in professional religious families. *Journal of Career Development* 12, 1 (September): 81–86. Upon review of the literature, the authors found that 75 percent of the clergy experience periods of major stress, and 33 percent have consequently considered leaving the ministry. Concludes that nonclergy spouses in particular have greater amounts of stress than nonmarried clergy.

Rioch, M. 1975. "All we like sheep—": Followers and leaders. *Group Relations Reader*, ed. A. D. Colman and W. H. Bexton. Sausalito, Calif.: GREX.

Rudnytsky, P. L. 1989. Winnicott and Freud. *Psychoanalytic Study of the Child* 44: 331–50. Examines the contrast between D. Winnicott's benevolent attitude toward religion and Freud's militant atheism by discussing similarities and differences in their upbringing and in their ideas on psychoanalysis.

Sappenfield, B. R. 1976. Belief in the omnipotency of love. *Psychological Reports* 38, 2: 399–402.

Satow, R. 1982. Response to Colleen Clements' "Misusing psychiatric models: The culture of narcissism." *Psychoanalytic Review* 69, 2: 296–302.

Schaef, A. W., and D. Fassel. 1988. *The addictive organization*. San Francisco: Harper and Row.

Scharfetter, C. 1983. Der Schamane—Das urbild des therapeuten. (The Shaman: Prototype of the therapist.) *Praxis der Psychotherapie und*

Psychosomatik 28, 2 (March): 81–89. Posits that the shamans were the original therapeutic entities and explores the shamans' relations to psychopathology and psychotherapy through ethological literature.

Schlauch, C. R. 1990. Illustrating two complementary enterprises at the interface of psychology and religion through reading Winnicott. *Pastoral Psychology* 39, 1 (September): 47–63. Examines D. Winnicott's (1986) article "Transitional objects and transitional phenomena" and focuses initially on the content of Winnicott's ideas and how they may be read in two different ways: as presenting psychology (which may be used in the psychology of religion) and as implicitly presenting religion-theology.

Schuller, D. S., M. P. Strommen, and M. L. Brekke, eds. 1981. *Ministry in America: A report and analysis, based on an in-depth survey of 47 denominations in the United States and Canada with interpretation by 18 experts.* San Francisco: Harper and Row.

Searles, H. F. 1990. The patient as therapist to his analyst. *Classics in Psychoanalytic Technique.* Northvale, N.J.: Jason Aronson.

Seidmann, P. 1978. Narcissus, the myth of self love and grandiosity. *Psychological Analysis* 9, 3: 202–12.

Serlin, I. 1989. A psycho-spiritual-body therapy approach to residential treatment of Catholic religious. *The Journal of Transpersonal Psychology* 21, 2: 177–91. Describes professional therapeutic work at a treatment center for Catholic clergy suffering from job stress and related emotional problems.

———. 1990. An activist's perspective: The inner nature of the environmental crisis. *Sierra Club, PA, US* 23, 2: 39–55. Argues that humanity's inability to find inner harmony is reflected in its inability to live in harmony with nature.

Shapiro, D. 1965. *Neurotic styles.* New York: Basic Books, Inc.

———. 1980. *Neurotic styles of personality.* New York: Jason Aronson.

Sheehy, Gail. 1974, 1976. *Passages.* New York: Dutton.

Shneidman, E. 1984. Personality and "success" among a selected group of lawyers. *Journal of Personality Assessment* 48, 6 (December): 609–16. Reveals that contentment, self-confidence, openness, spontaneity, cultural interests, freedom from hostility, and irritability were factors related to job success.

Slawson, Paul F. 1973. Treatment of a clergyman: Anxiety neurosis in a celibate. *American Journal of Psychotherapy* 27, 1 (January): 52–

60. Describes the treatment of a Roman Catholic priest who suffered progressive and almost debilitating anxiety when called upon to perform religious service.

Smith, Russell. Interview with author, 22 October 1984.

Snyder, D., R. M. Wills, and A. Grady-Fletcher. 1991. Risks and challenges of long-term psychotherapy outcome research: Reply to Jacobson. *Journal of Consulting and Clinical Psychology* 59, 1 (February): 146–49. Disputes N. S. Jacobson's (see PA 78:16162) characterizations of the behavioral marital therapy and insight-oriented marital therapy delivered in the D. K. Snyder, et al. comparative treatment study, and presents data to show that both treatments were as effective as or more so than previously published marital therapy outcome studies.

Sobo, S. 1977. Narcissism as a function of culture. *Psychoanalytic Study of the Child* 32: 155–72.

Sorensen, A. L. 1990. Psychoanalytic perspectives on religion: The illusion has a future. *Journal of Psychology and Theology* 18, 3 (Fall): 209–17. Several contemporary object relations theorists (e.g., D. W. Winnicott, 1971) have amended Freud's treatment of religion as exclusively pathological.

Steinke, P. 1989. Clergy affairs. *Journal of Psychology and Christianity* 8, 4 (Winter): 56–62. Examines clergy who have had affairs, and pinpoints four characteristics associated with this subgroup: projective identification; sex for nonsex purposes; need love; and unhealthy narcissism. Offers suggestions for prevention.

Stolorow, R. D. 1975. Toward a functional definition of narcissism. *International Journal of Psychoanalysis* 56, 2: 179–85.

Terkel, S. 1974. *Working: People talk about what they do all day and how they feel about what they do*. New York: Pantheon Books.

Thesaurus of Psychological Index Terms, 5th ed. 1988. American Psychological Assoc.

Tyler, A. 1985. *The accidental tourist*. New York: Knopf.

Vaillant, G. E. 1977. *Adaption to life*. Boston: Little, Brown and Co.

Wallace, E. 1983. Reflections on the relationship between psychoanalysis and Christianity. *Pastoral Psychology* 31, 4 (Summer): 215–43. Emphasizes that one's answer to the relationship between psychoanalysis and Christianity depends largely on one's conception of psychoanalysis. Some aspects of psychoanalytic theory and practice appear more reconcilable with Christian theology, ethics, and spirituality

182 BIBLIOGRAPHY

than others. A few psychoanalytic tenets seem directly to contradict religious ones.

Wallot, H., and J. Lambert. 1984. Characteristics of physician addicts. *American Journal of Drug and Alcohol Abuse* 10, 1: 53–62. Notes characteristics of addicted physicians: isolated, compliant, less outgoing, sexually inhibited, and more work- or academically oriented. However, the study acknowledges a diversity among physician addicts.

Warner, J., and J. Carter. 1984. Loneliness, marital adjustment and burnout in pastoral and lazy persons. *Journal of Psychology and Theology* 12, 2 (Summer): 125–31. Pastors and their spouses exhibited more loneliness and marital dysfunction as well as more symptoms of burnout compared to nonpastoral subjects and their spouses.

Watkins, D. C. 1977. Psychoanalytic object relation theory. Unpublished paper.

Weiser, C. W. 1983. Change: Summation effects hypothesis. Paper prepared for Susan Whelan, Temple University, Philadelphia, Pa., November.

———. 1984. The myth of equality and the hope for hope. Presentation to the collective multiple staffs of the National Lutheran Campus Ministry, Lake Forest College, Lake Forest, Ill., August 6–7.

———. 1985. Personality structure and success: A study of narcissism and related personality factors in successful Lutheran clergy. Temple University, Philadelphia. Microfilm.

Whitehead, B. D. 1993. Dan Quayle was right. *The Atlantic* 271, 4 (April): 47–50.

Whitfield, C. L. 1987 *Healing the child within: Discovery and recovery for adult children of dysfunctional families*. Pompano Beach, Fla.: Health Communications.

Wilkes, P. 1991. Profiles (Archbishop Weakland—Part II). *The New Yorker* (July 22): 46–65.

Wills, G. 1984. A personality study of musicians working in the popular field. *Personality and Individual Differences* 5, 3: 359–60. Reveals that popular musicians, as determined by the Eysenck Personality Questionnaire, demonstrated more of psychological disturbance than the general population.

Yalum, I. D. 1989. *Love's executioner and other tales of psychotherapy*. New York: Basic Books.

INDEX